THE BLESSED MOTHER'S PLAN TO SAVE HUMANITY

Marian Revelations and Necessity of Total Consecration

4th edition, revised

Jayson M. Brunelle

All references to Sacred Scripture in this book are taken from *The Holy Bible: Douay-Rheims version.* (2009). Charlotte, NC: St Benedict Press.

ISBN 978-146-8075069

Original artwork on the front cover is *The Virgin Mary in Prayer* by Sassoferrato, 17th Century.

Published by
Marian Apostolate Publishing
55 Maple St, Suite 8
Springfield, MA 01105
Email: marianapostolatepublishing@gmail.com
http://marianapostolate.wordpress.com

Printed in the United States of America.

DEDICATION

To the Sacred and Eucharistic Heart of Jesus: Refuge of Sinners, Consolation of the Afflicted, Sweetness and Delight of the Saints, Bread of Angels, Divine Physician and King of all Hearts.

To the Immaculate and Sorrowful Heart of Mary: Queen of Heaven and Earth, Queen of Peace; to whom the fate of humanity has been entrusted by the Most Holy Trinity.

To the Blessed Pope John Paul II the Great who, in consecrating his person, priesthood and papacy to the Blessed Virgin Mary, served as an exemplar of holiness for Christians the world over.

To my dearly beloved Jacqueline Marie Plank: my encouragement, support, source of inspiration, strength, dearest friend and soul-mate.

DECLARATIONS

Decree

The decree of the Congregation for the Propagation of the Faith, A.A.S.58, 1186 (approved by Pope Paul VI on October 14, 1966) states that the Nihil Obstat and Imprimatur are no longer required on publications that deal with private revelations, provided that they contain nothing contrary to faith and morals. The publisher recognizes and accepts that the final authority regarding the events described in this book rests with the Holy See of Rome, to whose judgment we willingly submit.

Pope Urban VIII

"In cases which concern private revelations, it is better to believe than not to believe, for if you believe and it is proven true, you will be happy that you have believed because our Holy Mother asked it. If you believe and it should be proven false, you will receive all blessings as if it had been true, because you believed it to be true" (Pope Urban VIII, 1623-44).

The *Catechism of the Catholic Church*

"Throughout the ages, there has been so-called "private revelations," some of which have been recognized by the authority of the Church. They do not belong, however, to the deposit of faith. It is not their role to improve or complete Christ's definite Revelation, but to *help live more fully by it* in a certain period of history. Guided by the magisterium of the church, the sensus fidelium knows how to discern and welcome in these revelations whatever constitutes an authentic call of Christ or of His saints to the Church" (p. 23, #67).

Sacred Scripture

"Do not quench the Spirit. Do not despise prophetic utterances. Test everything, retain what is good" (1 Thes. 5:19).

CONTENTS

INTRODUCTION

In 1977, Pope Paul VI wrote the following prophetic and apocalyptic sentiments that, in light of the countless Marian apparitions and revelations of the 20th Century, certainly apply to our times and to the content of this book:

"There is a great uneasiness, at this time, in the world and in the Church, and that which is in question is the faith. It so happens now that I repeat to myself the obscure phrase of Jesus in the Gospel of St. Luke: 'When the Son of Man returns, will He still find faith on the earth?' It so happens that there are books coming out in which the faith is in retreat on some important points, that the episcopates [bishops] are remaining silent and these books are not looked upon as strange. This, to me, is strange. I sometimes read the Gospel passage of the end times and I attest that, at this time, some signs of this end are emerging. Are we close to the end? This we will never know."

"We must always hold ourselves in readiness, but everything could last a very long time yet. What strikes me, when I think of the Catholic world, is that within Catholicism, there seems sometimes to predominate a non-Catholic way of thinking, and it can happen that this non-Catholic thought within Catholicism, will tomorrow become the stronger. But it will never represent the thought of the Church. It is necessary that a small flock subsist, no matter how small it might be" *(The Secret Paul VI* by Jean Guitton).

Moreover, this book was providentially finished on May 1, 2011, the great Feast of Divine Mercy Sunday, the beatification of Blessed John Paul II and the memorial of St. Joseph the Worker. This is of tremendous significance, both in itself and additionally for this book, as each of these feast days celebrates a mystery of the faith that has to do with the essential points in this book. John Paul not only instituted the Feast of Mercy as a liturgical feast to be celebrated on the second Sunday of Easter, but also passed on to his eternal reward on the vigil of that same feast in 2005. Additionally, as most know, Blessed John Paul II consecrated his life, priesthood and papacy to Mary, as indicated on his papal coat-of-arms and also in his papal motto *Totus Tuus*. Moreover, in the second section of this book, we explore the mystery of St. Joseph's profound sanctification as the logical consequence of his perfect and total consecration to the

Immaculate Heart of Mary through his spousal union with her, whereby a true exchange of hearts took place between them.

Thus, it was most appropriate that on the first day of May, the Month of Mary, which also happened to be the Feast of Divine Mercy and the memorial of St. Joseph, our truly great Pope John Paul II, the 263rd successor of Peter, responsible for ending the Cold War and ending communism in Poland, and who assiduously promoted a Marian Spirituality, was beatified. Moreover, this great pontiff worked zealously to spread devotion to the Divine Mercy merited by Christ as expressed in his encyclical letter, *Dives et Misericodia* (Rich in Mercy), which was certainly influenced by the writings of St. Faustina. Additionally, he recognized the significance and necessity of devotion to St. Joseph in our troubled times as expressed in the encyclical letter *Redemptoris Custos* (Guardian of the Redeemer). This truly great and holy man, who beatified 1,340 Blesseds and canonized 483 Saints, was himself numbered among those same Blessed by his immediate successor to the Chair of Peter, Pope Benedict XVI, and we earnestly pray that he be made a saint as soon as possible, as the crowds outside of St. Peter's Square chanted, upon learning of his passing, "Santo Subito!" – Sainthood now!

Blessed John Paul II, probably more than any other single person, understood the significance of the times in which he lived, the times in which we live. The end of the twentieth century and the beginning of the twenty-first century can truly be considered a prolonged, extended era of God's mercy within the climax of the age of Mary. But as Christ has foretold to numerous mystics, the time of Mercy will likely come to an end, to be followed by the era of God's Justice. When this occurs, the chastisements necessary for the purification of the Church and the world will constitute a time of great tribulation. In fact, many would argue, and this author would agree, that we have been living throughout a century of tribulation, as we see, with our own eyes, the "signs of the times," with the myriad catastrophes and cataclysms in nature, the rise of incurable diseases, famine, war and rumors of war, and so on. While it is true that this time in which we live is almost completely under the sign of the Antichrist, it is nonetheless true that these times are also and wonderfully under the sign of the "Woman clothed with the sun," that is, the Blessed Virgin Mary.

Like Blessed John Paul II, who, on so many occasions, entrusted his flock to the care of the Blessed Virgin Mary through solemn acts of consecration to her, I now solemnly entrust and consecrate this work to the maternal protection of the same Blessed Virgin Mary, imploring her to carry this little book into the hands of every soul who wishes to possess a greater understanding of both these times in which we live and Mary's perfect plan to rescue humanity from the clutches of the Evil One. May they use this knowledge to consecrate themselves to Mary and to earnestly live that consecration, that filial dependence on the Mother of God; to see with her eyes, to live with her life, to love with her Immaculate Heart, to be adorned with her virtues, to truly be her presence in the world to all whom they encounter, to pray and suffer in hiddenness, to be poor, chaste and humble, all with the intention of living the gospel to the letter for the greater glory of God and the salvation of souls.

May 1, 2011, Divine Mercy Sunday, Memorial of St. Joseph the Worker and the Solemn Beatification of Blessed Pope John Paul II.

1. MARY IN PRIVATE REVELATION

The Blessed Mother, in virtually every one of her Church-approved apparitions and messages to the world, has stated in no uncertain terms that humanity is on the brink of a massive, unprecedented chastisement, to be inflicted upon mankind in order to appease God's just wrath. Not only are we on the brink, but we are even now starting to witness, with all the cataclysms and catastrophes in nature, the times of the great "Tribulation." These messages are certainly apocalyptic in nature and are said to be unfolding as we speak. Mary states time and again to Fr. Gobbi of the Marian Movement of Priests - a Church approved association that boasts a membership of and endorsement by numerous cardinals, over 300 hundred bishops, over 60,000 priests and countless numbers of the laity – that we are living in the "latter-days," the "end-times" written about in Chapters 12 and 13 of St. John's Book of Revelation, which she explains in detail to Fr. Gobbi, and specifically, that we are currently living through a period sometimes referred to as the "Tribulation" and other times referred to as the "Purification." In what follows, I will attempt to assemble the many pieces of the Marian private revelation puzzle, formulating a picture of these unique times in which we live, and underscoring that throughout all of her messages, the most important, recurring theme is the Blessed Mother's ongoing request that humanity and each individual consecrate themselves to her Immaculate Heart, the sure refuge for our times.

Before we go any further, though, it should be noted that private revelation, as opposed to the definitive public revelation of God in the person of Jesus Christ, and which ended with the death last apostle John, never reveals anything new, but rather sheds a new light on certain truths of the deposit of faith as they apply concretely to the historical epoch in which the baptized live. This deposit of faith is safeguarded, preserved, and articulated by the Magisterium, the official teaching body of the Church. We, as Catholics, possess the fullness of God's Self-Revelation through the twin-fold source of Sacred Scripture and Sacred Tradition. Private revelations do, however, have their place in God's salvific plan for humanity. Speaking on the role of private revelation in the Church, the Catechism of the Catholic Church explains that, "Throughout the ages, there have been so-called "private" revelations, some of which have been recognized by the authority of the Church. They do not belong, however, to the deposit of faith. It is not their role to improve or complete Christ's definitive Revelation, but to help live more fully by it in a certain period of history" (CCC, Para. 67). Clearly, we are living in a definitive, critical time in human history, and the Blessed Mother has a plan to save humanity in general and each soul in particular, being Mother of the Mystical Body of Christ, the Church.

The Vision of Pope Leo XIII and Composition of the Prayer to St Michael

To put this in perspective, let us talk for a moment about a pivotal event that took place at the turn of the 19th to the 20th Century. It concerns Pope Leo XIII, who, by all accounts, was an extraordinarily holy man. For accuracy's sake, I shall here quote from a detailed and succinct account of what transpired:

"Exactly 33 years to the day prior to the great Miracle of the Sun in Fatima, that is, on October 13, 1884, Pope Leo XIII had a remarkable vision. When the aged Pontiff had finished celebrating Mass in his private Vatican Chapel, attended by a few Cardinals and members of the Vatican staff, he suddenly stopped at the foot of the altar. He stood there for about 10 minutes, as if in a trance, his face ashen white. Then, going immediately from the Chapel to his office, he composed the prayer to St. Michael, with instructions it be said after all Low Masses everywhere. When asked what had happened, he explained that, as he was about to leave the foot of the altar, he suddenly heard voices - two voices, one kind and gentle, the other guttural and harsh. They seemed to come from near the tabernacle. As he listened, he heard the following conversation: The guttural voice, the voice of Satan in his pride, boasted to Our Lord: "I can destroy your Church." The gentle voice of Our Lord: "You can? Then go ahead and do so." Satan: "To do so, I need more time and more power." Our Lord: "How much time? How much power?" Satan: "75 to 100 years, and a greater power over those who will give themselves over to my service." Our Lord: "You have the time, you will have the power. Do with them what you will" (*The Vision of Pope Leo XIII*, 2011).

As we know, this period of 100 years granted by God to Satan to tempt humanity and to put it to, as it were, the "final test," constitutes the 20th Century. Is it any wonder, then, that at this point in history, the end of the 20th Century and the very beginning of the 21st Century, the Blessed Mother is appearing all over the world, pleading for the consecration of all to Her Immaculate Heart, the safe refuge in these times of the apostasy and the great rejection of God and His law of love?

The Pivotal Event of Fatima

In 1917 the Blessed Mother appeared to the three shepherd-children of Fatima, Jacinta, Francisco and Lucia. She came with three secrets which contained prophetic and dire warnings regarding the 20th Century. The first secret consisted of a terrifying vision of hell. The second secret reads as follows:

"You have seen hell where the souls of poor sinners go. To save them, God wishes to establish in the world devotion to my Immaculate Heart. If what I say to you is done, many souls will be saved and there will be peace. The war is going to end: but if people do not cease offending God, a worse one will break out during the Pontificate of Pope Pius XI. When you see a night illumined by an unknown light, know that this is the great sign given you by God that he is about to punish the world for its crimes, by means of war, famine, and persecutions of the Church and of the Holy Father. To prevent this, I shall come to ask for the Consecration of Russia to my Immaculate Heart, and the Communion of reparation on the First Saturdays. If my requests are heeded, Russia will be converted, and there will be peace; if not, she will spread her errors throughout the world, causing wars and persecutions of the Church. The good will be martyred; the Holy Father will have much to suffer; various nations will be annihilated. In the end, my Immaculate Heart will triumph. The Holy Father will consecrate Russia to me, and she shall be converted, and a period of peace will be granted to the world" (*The Secret in Three Parts: The Second Part*, 2010).

In the above secret, one of the most important lines is the second when she states, "You have seen hell where the souls of poor sinners go. To save them, God wishes to establish in the world devotion to my Immaculate Heart." It is through the perfect devotion of Total Consecration to Mary's Immaculate Heart that individuals and, ultimately, the world, will be saved, and the promised Triumph of Mary's Immaculate Heart will take place. It is this author's opinion that the messages given to Fr. Gobbi of the Marian Movement of Priests coupled with the phenomenon of Medjugorje, which is still under Church investigation at the time of this writing, constitute the completion and fulfillment of the messages and secrets given at Fatima. The theme of the Marian Movement of Priests' collected messages is specifically the spreading of devotion to Mary's Immaculate Heart by encouraging all, priests and laity, to consecrate themselves to Her Heart through a formal act, and then to live that consecration. According to the messages given to Fr. Gobbi, she promises two things to those who entrust themselves to her through a solemn act of consecration: these souls shall not fall prey to any of the numerous theological and philosophical errors being promoted in our times; that is to say, they will remain faithful to the Gospel and will be preserved in the true Catholic faith; and second, they will not perish; that is, their salvation is assured.

Medjugorje, as compared to the Marian Movement of Priests, is more of a clarion call for the masses. The Blessed mother knows her audience; while the messages of Mary to Fr. Gobbi are oriented primarily for well educated, theologically-trained priests, and, for that reason, use high theological language, the messages given to the visionaries of Medjugorje are very short and use simple language that persons from all walks of life – educated or not – can comprehend. In short, she is reaching out to all of her spiritual children, regardless of their vocation, age, race, ethnicity, religious affiliation or education level.

The Current State of Affairs

Satan has succeeded in His plan of seducing the nations, using both the West and the East. The West is not without fault – exerting, as it does, so much influence in and throughout the world. It has successfully exported to the world it's satanic ideals of unbridled capitalism, hedonism, and a perverted use of freedom to worship the false idol of the ego. Hate amongst individuals evolves into hate amongst nations, and crime, violence, war and disaster are the consequence for mankind. Additionally, the East is exporting and seducing many nations through Marxist Atheism, referred to by Our Mother in Fr. Gobbi's book as the "huge Red Dragon" of the Book of Revelation. Thus, we are witnessing the final phase of the battle between the "Woman clothed with the sun" and the "huge Red Dragon," which is Marxist Atheism, which results in the great, world-wide apostasy through which we are now living. This reality should be the most pressing concern on our collective consciousness, as the fate of humanity in general and each human soul in particular is at stake.

God is not simply speaking to us through the revelations of the Virgin. Additionally, He is speaking through the upheavals in nature, wars, a dramatic rise in incurable diseases, and so on. We witness, from day-to-day, unprecedented natural cataclysms and catastrophes, such as the world has not seen since the time of the deluge in the Old Testament. Realistically, how can we argue against the Blessed Virgin Mary when She states, through Father Gobbi, that we are, in fact, living through the "Great Tribulation?" Finally, Mother Mary states in her messages to Fr.

Gobbi and to others that the times through which we are living are much worse than the times of Noah, and that she has been holding back the just right arm of the Father's wrath by offering him first, the Blood of Jesus and second, the prayer and suffering of so many specially chosen "victim-souls" here on Earth, who have made a solemn consecration of their lives to her, a consecration which enables her to fully exercise her role as Mediatrix of all Graces with respect to the consecrated soul. Thus, it is through the Blood, Passion, Death and Resurrection of Jesus Christ, coupled with the prayers and sufferings of her little faithful remnant, that Mary is holding back the wrath of the Father.

Simply put, God is quite angry with humanity, and, in his infinite justice, demands that humanity repent of its evil ways and return to Him via prayer and penance. He's been sending Mary, the "Woman" who begins Scripture in the Book of Genesis and ends scripture in the Book of Revelation. Long before Fatima, the Triumph of the Woman was foretold at the very beginning of Scripture, in the proto-evangelium – the first gospel, or the promise of salvation - in Genesis 3:15: "Behold, I will put enmity between you and the Woman, between your seed and Hers. She will crush your head, and you will bite at her heel," and again, at the very end of Scripture, Chapter 12 of the Book of Revelation: "There appeared a great sign in the sky – a Woman, clothed with the sun, with the moon under her feet, and on her head a crown of twelve stars." She and the Dragon, Her faithful cohort and his, do battle with each other. Thus, a truly cosmic battle is taking place between the "Woman clothed with the sun" and "the great Red Dragon," and human souls are the casualties. Wonderfully, the final outcome has already been established: As She stated at Fatima and reiterates to Fr. Gobbi and additionally in many of her Church-approved private revelations, in the end, Her Immaculate Heart will Triumph. The Woman, with her faithful cohort of children consecrated totally to her, will defeat the Red Dragon, the Ancient Serpent, who is the Devil and Satan. For, as she predicted in Fatima, "In the end, my Immaculate Heart will triumph." She will bind Satan with the frail cord of the Rosary and shut him up in hell, and he will not be permitted to attack humanity any longer.

The Call

Mary has been pleading, in allher apparitions and messages, for the world to return to God through fervent prayer and penance. Yet humanity is largely ignoring Her. The anti-supernatural, mainstream media refuses to report on the numerous miraculous, scientifically inexplicable events that have been transpiring all throughout the 20th century, especially during its latter half, when Marian apparitions, messages, warnings, secrets, and miracles took on a great and unprecedented momentum. Quite simply, we are living in the "Age of Mary." Just as Mary was chosen by the Father to precede the first coming of Christ, she is likewise preceding the Second Glorious Coming of Jesus. The Blessed Mother has stated, as have numerous saints and theologians, that the Mystical Body of Christ, or the Church itself, must undergo, like Christ, a passion and crucifixion. Also in imitation of Christ, its head, it shall rise in luminous glory, and a "new springtime" for the Church and the world will constitute the culmination of the Blessed Mother's plan to save humanity: a "new springtime" to be ushered in by the Triumph of Mary's Immaculate Heart in the world, which, according to the revelations given to Fr. Gobbi, will coincide with the Second Glorious Coming of Christ.

Despite the good news of Mary's ultimate Triumph, however, Mary's dire warnings and her great plea to humanity to soften God's anger via prayer and suffering/penance is largely going unheeded. This potential chastisement that can be mitigated, if not eliminated, of "fire falling from the sky," wiping out a significant portion of the population, is not being taken seriously by mankind, with the exception of that faithful remnant of children consecrated totally to their spiritual Mother Mary. Mainstream persons refuse to pay her any attention and continue down their diabolical path of hatred, egoism, hedonism, materialism, moral relativism and self and other destruction. If, on the other hand, we can do our part by entrusting ourselves to the safe refuge of the Immaculate Heart of Mary through our formal and lived-out consecration to her, we may be able to significantly mitigate the chastisement – a chastisement that will only come if the Father's demand for justice through prayer and penance is not met.

As we read these apocalyptic messages, certain recurring, major themes emerge and we are capable of piecing together Mary's plan to save humanity. Two things are certain: God's mercy will come to an end, and His demand for justice through suffering will be met; through the suffering of the potential chastisement, coupled with and mitigated by the heroic prayer and suffering of Mary's consecrated priests and laypersons, the "faithful remnant," that the Church and the world will be purified and renewed, ushering in the Triumph of the Immaculate Heart of Mary and the coinciding Second Glorious Coming of Jesus. Thereby establishing "the new heavens and the new earth," and bringing to fulfillment that which Our Lord instructed us to pray for in the Our Father prayer: "Thy Kingdom come, Thy will be done, on earth as it is in heaven."

2. RECURRING THEMES IN MARY'S PROPHETIC MESSAGES

Let us, then, take a closer look at some of the recurring themes that manifest throughout certain of the pivotal Church-approved private revelations of Mary. Through a careful reading of five key prophecies concerning these, the "latter times," along with the tremendous insights afforded us through Mary's locutions to Fr. Gobbi (*To the Priests, Our Lady's Beloved Sons*, a collection of interior locutions from Mary that not only has the Imprimatur but also the endorsement of Bernardino Cardinal Echeverria Ruiz, O.F.M., Archbishop Emeritus of Guayaquil, and a second Imprimatur by Donald W. Montrose, D.D., Bishop of Stockton), we should be able to make some sense of the many events that are occurring both within the Church and throughout the world.

A Great Chastisement Will Befall Humanity

The best way of introducing this topic is simply to reproduce these most important messages and the contents of the Church-approved "secrets," disclosed to the seers and visionaries and told to Vatican Officials, who have now made these messages partially or completely public. In this section, the messages of Fatima, Akita, La Salette, the Lady of All Nations and the interior locutions received by Don Steffano Gobbi will be reprinted and commented on. Using a minor form of discourse analysis with public archival data, let us examine the common themes that emerge by closely reading through and comparing the text of these Church-approved messages.

It is my hope that the reader will prayerfully meditate on (1) these messages; (2) the theology of Marian consecration; (3) and the essays on how to live the consecration, specifically, the essay on the Eucharist. These supernatural messages, or "private" revelations should not be taken lightly or for granted; they were given to humanity and approved by the Church for a great purpose that pertains specifically to the times in which we live, and we should consider it an honor to have, at our very fingertips, the contents of these heavenly messages. Due to the profound import of each of these messages, they shall be reproduced here in their entirety. Some messages are clearer than others. It should be noted that prophecy tends to be cryptic and highly symbolic, as is the case with each of the secrets. We must remember that, oftentimes, it is only in hindsight that we can fully make sense of these prophesies. To begin, let us turn our attention to the text of the Third Secret of Fatima.

Text of the Third Secret of Fatima

"I write in obedience to you, my God, who command me to do so through his Excellency the Bishop of Leiria and through your Most Holy Mother and mine. After the two parts which I have already explained, at the left of Our Lady and a little above, we saw an Angel with a flaming sword in his left hand; flashing, it gave out flames that looked as though they would set the world on fire; but they died out in contact with the splendour that Our Lady radiated towards him from her right hand: pointing to the earth with his right hand, the Angel cried out in a loud voice: 'Penance, Penance, Penance!.' And we saw in an immense light that is God: 'something similar to how people appear in a mirror when they pass in front of it' a Bishop dressed in White 'we had the impression that it was the Holy Father'. Other Bishops, Priests, men and women Religious going up a steep mountain, at the top of which there was a big Cross of rough-hewn trunks as of a cork-tree with the bark; before reaching there the Holy Father passed through a big city half in ruins and half trembling with halting step, afflicted with pain and sorrow, he prayed for the souls of the corpses he met on his way; having reached the top of the mountain, on his knees at the foot of the big Cross he was killed by a group of soldiers who fired bullets and arrows at him, and in the same way there died one after another the other Bishops, Priests, men and women Religious, and various lay people of different ranks and positions. Beneath the two arms of the Cross there were two Angels each with a crystal aspersorium in his hand, in which they gathered up the blood of the Martyrs and with it sprinkled the souls that were making their way to God" (*The Message of Fatima, Congregaton of the Doctrine of the Faith*, 2000).

The Third Secret is probably the clearest of the three I have here reproduced. At the beginning, we see the Angel of God's justice with a "flaming sword" that "Flashing, it gave out flames that looked as though they would set the world on fire; but they died out in contact with the splendor that Our Lady radiated toward him from her right hand." As we shall see in the next message, the visionary Sr. Agnes states that in the vision she saw, if humanity did not repent, a great chastisement of "fire falling from the sky, wiping out a great portion of humanity" would be the consequence. The Fatima message seems to hold out the hope that Our Lady will deflect these flames from heaven. This she shall do by offering to the Father the Precious Blood of Jesus coupled with the prayer and penance of her chosen victim-souls, those consecrated to her.

The Angel cries out, "Penance, Penance, Penance!" Three is a most significant, sacred number, as it represents the Most Holy Trinity. We must atone for our sins against the Father, the Son and the Holy Spirit. Next they saw an "immense light that is God: something similar to how people appear in a mirror when they pass in front of it." This clearly seems to indicate the world-wide warning spoken of by so many other visionaries. Essentially, the warning will be one of the greatest acts of God's mercy in that He will allow each human person on the planet to see, in an instant, the sinful state of their souls in the burning light and fire of His divine truth. It will result in a mass conversion. We shall discuss this great "illumination of Conscience" in future chapters.

The remainder of the message is fairly obscure, but is does seem to resonate with other similar messages that predict a bloody persecution of the faithful, with a serious attack being made on a Pope's life. Many, including Cardinal Sodano, say that the failed assassination attempt on the life of Pope John Paul II was predicted in this message, and that very well seems to be the case, as the shooting took place on May 13, 1981, the Feast of Our Lady of Fatima! Clearly, Our Lady intervened and saved his life on that day. After all, he did officially consecrated his life, priesthood and papacy to her Immaculate Heart, as is depicted in his papal motto, *Totus Tuus* (Mother, I am totally yours) and represented on his papal coat-of-arms. Moreover, while in the hospital recuperating from the attack on his life, he specifically asked that the then unrevealed Third Secret of Fatima be brought to him for him to read and reflect upon. And he did state that he owed his life to Our Lady of Fatima. Moreover, Our Lady, in a messages entitled, "The Pope of My Secret," given via interior locution to Fr. Gobbi, states the following: "You are aware of being spiritually very much united with my Pope, John Paul II, this precious gift which my Immaculate Heart has made to you, who, in these very moments, is in prayer at the Cova da Iria, to thank me for the motherly and extraordinary protection which I gave him, by saving his life, on the occasion of the bloody attempt made upon it, which took place…in St. Peter's Square. Today I confirm for you that this is the pope of my secret, the Pope about whom I spoke to the children during the apparitions, the Pope of my love and my sorrow" (Gobbi, Message 449, Para. B-C). Thus, Blessed John Paul II was a gift to the Church for these times and played an instrumental role in the Blessed Mother's plan to save humanity.

The Apparitions to Sr. Agnes Sasagawa of Akita

The following excerpt has been reproduced from www.ewtn.com: "The extraordinary events began on June 12, 1973, when Sr. Agnes saw brilliant mysterious rays emanate suddenly from the tabernacle. The same thing happened on each of the two days that followed.

"On June 28, 1973, a cross-shaped wound appeared on the inside left hand of Sr. Agnes. It bled profusely and caused her much pain. On July 6, Sr. Agnes heard a voice coming from the statue of the Blessed Virgin Mary in the chapel where she was praying. The statue was carved from a single block of wood from a Katsura tree and is three feet tall. On the same day, a few of the sisters noticed drops of blood flowing from the statue's right hand. On four occasions, this act of blood flow repeated itself. The wound in the statue's hand remained until September 29, when it disappeared. On September 29, the day the wound on the statue disappeared, the sisters noticed the statue had now begun to "sweat", especially on the forehead and neck. On August 3, Sr. Agnes received a second message. On October 13, she received a final third message. "Two years later on January 4, 1975, the statue of the Blessed Virgin began to weep. It continued to weep at intervals for the next 6 years and eight months. It wept on 101 occasions."

Chronology of the Church's Approval of Akita

"April, 1984—Most. Rev. John Shojiro Ito, Bishop of Niigata, Japan, after years of extensive investigation, declares the events of Akita, Japan to be of supernatural origin, and authorizes throughout the entire diocese the veneration of the Holy Mother of Akita"
(www.ewtn.com/library/mary/akita.htm).

"On April 22, 1984, after eight years of investigations, after consultation with the Holy See, the messages of Our Lady of Akita were approved by the Bishop of the diocese. In the Japanese village of Akita, a statue of the Madonna, according to the testimony of more than 500 Christians and non-Christians, including the Buddhist mayor of the town, has shed blood, sweat and tears. A nun, Agnes Katsuko Sasagawa has received the stigmata and has received messages from Our Lady" (*ibid.*).

"June, 1988—Vatican City—Joseph Cardinal Ratzinger, Prefect, Congregation for the Doctrine of the Faith, gives definitive judgement on the Akita events and messages as reliable and worthy of belief" (*ibid.*).

Text of the Message of Akita

"Many men in this world afflict the Lord. I desire souls to console Him to soften the anger of the Heavenly Father. I wish, with My Son, for souls who will repair, by their suffering and their poverty, for the sinners and ingrates. In order that the world might know His anger, the Heavenly Father is preparing to inflict a great chastisement on all mankind. With My Son, I have intervened so many times to appease the wrath of the Father. I have prevented the coming of calamities by offering Him the sufferings of the Son on the Cross, His Precious Blood, and beloved souls who (www.ewtn.com/library/MARY/AKITA.HTM).

"If men do not repent and better themselves, the Father will inflict a terrible punishment on all humanity. It will be a punishment greater than the deluge, such as one will never have seen before. Fire will fall from the sky and will wipe out a great part of humanity, the good as well as the bad, sparing neither priests nor faithful. The survivors will find themselves so desolate that they will envy the dead. The only arms which will remain for you will be the Rosary and the Sign left by My Son. Each day recite the prayers of the Rosary. With the Rosary, pray for the Pope, the Bishops and the priests" (*ibid.*).

"The work of the devil will infiltrate even into the Church in such a way that one will see Cardinals opposing Cardinals, Bishops against other Bishops. The priests who venerate Me will be scorned and opposed by their confreres (other priests). Churches and altars will be sacked. The Church will be full of those who accept compromises, and the demon will press many priests and consecrated souls to leave the service of the Lord. The demon will be especially implacable against the souls consecrated to God. The thought of the loss of so many souls is the cause of My sadness. If sins increase in number and gravity, there will no longer be pardon for them...Pray very much the prayers of the Rosary. I alone am able to still save you from the calamities which approach. Those who place their confidence in Me will be saved" (*ibid.*).

Reflection on the Message of Akita

The messages of Akita are so similar to the secrets of Fatima that Pope Benedict, when he was Cardinal, confirmed that the two messages were essentially the same. Moreover, Sr. Agnes received her third message on October 13, the anniversary of the miracle of the sun at Fatima. Here, again, we have the theme of a great chastisement that is conditional, pending the return of humanity to God and the offering of prayer (especially the Holy Rosary) and penance (specifically, the daily carrying of one's cross with a spirit of patience, resignation of will and humility). Again, the Blessed Mother speaks of appeasing the wrath of the Father by offering the Passion of her son, together with the prayers and sufferings of her victim-souls.

Moreover, she prophetically speaks of Satan infiltrating into the summit of the Church, that is to say, the hierarchy, with "Cardinals opposing Cardinals, Bishops against other Bishops." Finally she states, "The priests who venerate Me will be scorned and opposed by their confreres (other priests). Churches and altars will be sacked. The Church will be full of those who accept compromises, and the demon will press many priests and consecrated souls to leave the service of the Lord." Clearly, Satan is striking the Church in an unprecedented fashion. She indicates that there will be persecution of the Church both from within and from without. As we continue on in our investigation of Marian revelations, this theme of internal and external persecution of the Church will be made clear. Finally, Our Lady, to Sr. Agnes, calls for the praying of the Rosary. This is a constant, recurring theme running throughout almost every single Marian apparition. Let us, then, pick up our Rosaries and pray them each day, without fail, as the daily renewal of our total consecration.

The Approved Private Revelation of La Salette

The message was approved by the Catholic Church and published in its entirety at Lecce, France, on November 15, 1979 with the imprimatur of Bishop Zola. The following excerpt is quoted from *The Catholic Encyclopedia* at www.newadvent.org

"La Salette, in the commune and parish of La Salette-Fallavaux, Canton of Corps, Department of Isere, and Diocese of Grenoble. It is celebrated as the place where… the Blessed Virgin appeared to two little shepherds; and each year is visited by a large number of pilgrims. On 19 September, 1846, about three o'clock in the afternoon in full sunlight, on a mountain about 5918 feet high and about three miles distant from the village of La Salette-Fallavaux, it is related that two children, a shepherdess of fifteen named Melanie Calvat, called Mathieu, and a shepherd-boy of eleven named Maximin Giraud, both of them very ignorant, beheld in a resplendent light a "beautiful lady" clad in a strange costume. Speaking alternately in French and in patois, she charged them with a message which they were "to deliver to all her people." After complaining of the impiety of Christians, and threatening them with dreadful chastisements in case they should persevere in evil, she promised them the Divine mercy if they would amend" (www.newadvent.org/cathen/09008b.htm).

Text of the Message of La Salette

"Melanie, what I am about to tell you now will not always be a secret. You may make it public in 1858. The priests, ministers of my Son, the priests, by their wicked lives, by their irreverence and their impiety in the celebration of the holy mysteries, by their love of money, their love of honors and pleasures, the priests have become cesspools of impurity. Yes, the priests are asking for vengeance, and vengeance is hanging over their heads. Woe to the priests and to those consecrated to God who by their infidelity and their wicked lives are crucifying My Son again! The sins of those dedicated to God cry out towards Heaven and call for vengeance, and now vengeance is at their door, for there is no one left to beg mercy and forgiveness for the people. There are no more generous souls; there is no one left worthy of offering a spotless sacrifice to the Eternal for the sake of the world. God will strike in an unprecedented way. Woe to the inhabitants of the earth! God will exhaust His wrath upon them, and no one will be able to escape so many afflictions together" (www.catholicapologetics.info/catholicteaching/privaterevelation/lasalet. html).

"The chiefs, the leaders of the people of God have neglected prayer and penance, and the devil has bedimmed their intelligence. They have become wandering stars which the old devil will drag along with his tail to make them perish. God will allow the old serpent to cause divisions among those who reign, in every society and in every family. Physical and moral agonies will be suffered. God will abandon mankind to itself and will send punishments which will follow one after the other for more than thirty-five years. The society of men is on the eve of the most terrible scourges and of gravest events. Mankind must expect to be ruled with an iron rod and to drink from the chalice of the wrath of God. May the vicar of my Son, Pope Pius IX, never leave Rome again after 1859; may he, however, be steadfast and noble, may he fight with the weapons of faith and love. I will be at his side. May he be on his guard against Napoleon: he is two-faced, and when he wishes to make himself Pope as well as Emperor, soon God will draw back from him. He is the eagle who, always wanting to ascend further, will fall on the sword he wished to use to force his people to be raised up" (*ibid.*).

"Italy will be punished for her ambition in wanting to shake off the yoke of the Lord of Lords. And so she will be left to fight a war; blood will flow on all sides. Churches will be locked up or desecrated. Priests and religious orders will be hunted down, and made to die a cruel death. Several will abandon the Faith, and a great number of priests and members of religious orders will break away from the true religion; among these people there will even be bishops. May the Pope guard against the performers of miracles. For the time has come when the most astonishing wonders will take place on the earth and in the air" (*ibid.*).

"In the year 1864, Lucifer together with a large number of demons will be unloosed from hell; they will put an end to faith little by little, even in those dedicated to God. They will blind them in such a way, that, unless they are blessed with a special grace, these people will take on the spirit of these angels of hell; several religious institutions will lose all faith and will lose many souls. Evil books will be abundant on earth and the spirits of darkness will spread everywhere a universal slackening in all that concerns the service of God. They will have great power over nature: there will be churches built to serve these spirits. People will be transported from one place to another by these evil spirits, even priests, for they will not have been guided by the good spirit of the Gospel, which is a spirit of humility, charity and zeal for the glory of God. On occasions, the dead and the righteous will be brought back to life" (*ibid.*).

"In all places there will be extraordinary wonders, because the true faith has died and a false light shines on the world. Woe to the princes of the Church whose only occupation will be to heap wealth upon more wealth, and to preserve their authority and proud domination! The vicar of my Son will have much to suffer, as, for a time, the Church will be the victim of great persecution: this will be the time of darkness. The Church will suffer a terrible crisis. As the holy Faith of God is forgotten, every individual will wish to be his own guide and be superior to his fellow-men. Civil and Ecclesiastical authority will be abolished. All order and all justice will be trampled underfoot. Nothing will be seen but murder, hatred, jealousy, falsehood and discord without love for the mother country or for the family" (*ibid.*).

"The Holy Father will suffer a greatly. I will be at his side to the end in order to receive his sacrifice. The wicked will make several attempts on his life, but they cannot harm him. But neither he nor his successor will live to see the triumph of the Church of God. All the civil governments will have one and the same plan, which will be to abolish and do away with every religious principle, to make way for materialism, atheism, spiritualism and vice of all kinds" (*ibid.*).

"In the year 1865, there will be desecration of holy places. In convents, the flowers of the Church will decompose and the devil will make himself like the king of all hearts. May those in charge of religious communities be on their guard against the people they must receive, for the devil will resort to all his evil tricks to introduce sinners into religious orders, for disorder and the love of carnal pleasures will be spread all over the earth. France, Italy, Spain and England will be at war. Blood will flow in the streets. Frenchman will fight Frenchman, Italian will fight Italian. A general war will follow which will be appalling. For a time, God will cease to remember France and Italy because the Gospel of Jesus Christ has been forgotten. The wicked will make use of all their evil ways. Men will kill each other; massacre each other even in their homes" (*ibid.*).

"At the first blow of His thundering sword, the mountains and all nature will tremble in terror, for the disorders and crimes of men have pierced the vault of the heavens. Paris will burn and Marseilles will be engulfed. Several cities will be shaken down and swallowed up by earthquakes. People will believe that all is lost. Nothing will be seen but murder, nothing will be heard but the clash of arms and blasphemy. The righteous will suffer greatly. Their prayers, their penance and their tears will rise up to Heaven and all of God's people will beg for forgiveness and mercy and will plead for My help and intercession. And then Jesus Christ, in an act of His justice and His great mercy will command His angels to have all His enemies put to death" (*ibid.*).

"Suddenly, the persecutors of the Church of Jesus Christ and all those given over to sin will perish and the earth will become desert-like. And then peace will be made, and man will be reconciled with God. Jesus Christ will be served, worshipped, and glorified. Charity will flourish everywhere. The new kings will be the right arm of the Holy Church, which will be strong, humble, pious in its poor but fervent in the imitation of the virtues of Jesus Christ. The Gospel will be preached everywhere and mankind will make great progress in its Faith, for there will be unity among the workers of Jesus Christ and man will live in fear of God. This peace among men will be short-lived. Twenty-five years of plentiful harvests will make them forget that the sins of men are the cause of all the troubles on this earth" (*ibid.*).

"A forerunner of the Antichrist, with his troops gathered from several nations, will fight against the true Christ, the only Savior of the world. He will shed much blood and will want to annihilate the worship of God to make himself be looked upon as a god. The earth will be struck by calamities of all kinds (in addition to plague and famine which will be widespread). There will be a series of wars until the last war, which will then be fought by the ten kings of the Antichrist, all of whom will have one and the same plan and will be the only rulers of the world. Before this comes to pass, there will be a kind of false peace in the world. People will think of nothing but amusement. The wicked will give themselves over to all kinds of sin. But the children of the Holy Church, the children of the Faith, my true followers, they will grow in their love for God and in all the virtues most precious to Me. Blessed are the souls humbly guided by the Holy Spirit! I shall fight at their side until they reach a fullness of years" (*ibid.*).

"Nature is asking for vengeance because of man, and she trembles with dread at what must happen to the earth stained with crime. Tremble, earth, and you who proclaim yourselves as serving Jesus Christ and who, on the inside, only adore yourselves, tremble, for God will hand you over to His enemy because the holy places are in the state of corruption. Many convents are no longer houses of God, but the grazing-grounds of Asmodeus and his like. It will be during this time that the Antichrist will be born of a Hebrew nun, a false virgin who will communicate with the old serpent, the master of impurity, his father will be Bishop. At birth he will spew out blasphemy; he will have teeth, in a word, he will be the devil incarnate. He will scream horribly, he will perform wonders, he will feed on nothing but impurity. He will have brothers who, although not devils incarnate like him, will be children of evil. At the age of twelve, they will draw attention upon themselves by the gallant victories they will have won; soon they will each lead armies, aided by the legions of hell" (*ibid.*).

"The seasons will be altered, the earth will produce nothing but bad fruit, the stars will lose their regular motion, and the moon will only reflect a faint reddish glow. Water and fire will give the earth's globe convulsions and terrible earthquakes which will swallow up mountains, cities. Rome will lose the faith and become the seat of the Antichrist. The demons of the air together with the Antichrist will perform great wonders on earth and in the atmosphere, and men will become more and more perverted. God will take care of his faithful servants and men of good will. The Gospel will be preached everywhere, and all peoples of all nations will get to know the truth" (*ibid.*).

"I make an urgent appeal to the earth. I call on the true disciples of the living God who reigns in Heaven; I call on the true followers of Christ made man, the only true Savior of men; I call on My children, the true faithful, those who have given themselves to Me so that I may lead them to My Divine Son, those whom I carry in My arms, so to speak, those who have lived according to My spirit. Finally, I call on the Apostles of the Last Days, the faithful disciples of Jesus Christ who have lived in scorn for the world and for themselves, in poverty and in humility, in scorn and in silence, in prayer and in mortification, in chastity and in union with God, in suffering and unknown to the world. It is time they came out and filled the world with light. Go and reveal yourselves to be my cherished children. I am at your side and within you, provided that your faith is the light which shines upon you in these unhappy days. May your zeal make you hunger for the glory and the honor of Jesus Christ. Fight, children of light, you, the few who can see. For now is the time of all times, the end of all ends" (*ibid.*).

"The Church will be in eclipse, the world will be in dismay. But now Enoch and Eli will come, filled with the Spirit of God. They will preach with the might of God, and men of good will believe in God, and many souls will be comforted. They will make great strides forward through the virtue of the Holy Spirit, and will condemn the diabolical errors of the Antichrist. Woe to the inhabitants of the earth! There will be bloody wars and famines, plagues and infectious diseases. It will rain with a fearful hail of animals. There will be thunderstorms which will shake cities, earthquakes which will swallow up countries. Voices will be heard in the air. Men will beat their heads against walls, call for their death, and on the other hand death will be their torment. Blood will flow on all sides. Who will be the victor if God does not shorten the duration of the test? At the blood, the tears and the prayers of the righteous, God will relent. Enoch and Eli will be put to death. Pagan Rome will disappear. The fire of Heaven will fall and consume three cities. All the universe will be struck with terror and many will let themselves be led astray, because they have not worshipped the true Christ who lives among them. It is time; the sun is darkening; only faith will survive" (*ibid.*).

"Now is the time, the abyss is opening. Here is the king of kings of darkness, here is the Beast with his subjects, calling himself the Savior of the world. He will rise proudly into the air to go to Heaven. He will be smothered by the breath of the Archangel Saint Michael. He will fall, and the earth, which will have been in a continual series of evolutions for three days, will open up its fiery bowels; and he will have plunged for eternity with all his followers into the everlasting chasms of hell. And then water and fire will purge the earth and consume all the works of men's pride and all will be renewed. God will be served and glorified" (*ibid.*).

Reflection on the Message of La Salette

The beginning of this quite long and sometimes difficult to understand prophecy has to do with a quote from the book of the Apocalypse, where it speaks of the beast's tail wiping a third of the stars out of the firmament of heaven. Our Blessed Mother has revealed in other messages, such as those given to Fr. Gobbi, that the priests are the shining stars, the beloved sons of Mary who, under the influence of the evil one, have allowed themselves to become corrupted, seeking after earthly and carnal pleasures, consumed with greed for money, prestige and power. According to this revelation, the sins of the priests and consecrated souls cry out for vengeance to God, and accordingly, they should tremble with fear of what God has in store for them. The recent sex-abuse scandal within the Church has brought to light some very unsavory characteristics of men who are supposed to be among the most trustworthy, men who have freely dedicated themselves to the service of God and who, despite their exalted vocation and calling, have given themselves over to the evil one. The heavenly Father's cup of justice is full to overflowing, and has been for some time now. Thus, this revelation is a clarion call to priests and consecrated souls to turn back to the service of God, to convert, to entrust themselves to the Blessed Mother through consecration to her, in order to amend their lives, atone for the sins of their lives and be spared the eternal torments of hell.

Yet again she speaks of a great chastisement, she seems to predict the two World Wars, and she speaks about the apostles of the end times. Of these latter, she speaks of how they shall be imbued with her spirit, having entrusted themselves completely to her in order to be brought most perfectly to her Son, Jesus. Thus again, in this message, the importance of individual consecration to the Immaculate heart is underscored. The theme of the apostasy is also touched upon here, as the Blessed Mother states that in 1864, demonic spirits would be unleashed upon the earth to bring about loss of the true faith. Unless people are given a "special grace," which is the grace that comes with being consecrated to Our Lady, they will invariably become victims of error and the apostasy.

Then there is this passage from the text of the message: "'The Holy Father will suffer a greatly. I will be at his side to the end in order to receive his sacrifice. The wicked will make several attempts on his life, but they cannot harm him. But neither he nor his successor will live to see the triumph of the Church of God." This author has become convinced that when the Blessed Mother speaks about "the Holy Father" in her messages, unless she clearly indicates otherwise, she is likely speaking about Blessed John Paul II. Attempts were made on his life, and he battled a long, painful struggle with Parkinson's disease toward the end. Moreover, he died on the vigil of Divine Mercy Sunday, a great feast within the Church that he not only officially instituted, but that he was involved in at every significant step of the way (in terms of Sr. Faustina's writings, her eventual beatification and ultimately, her canonization – along with official approbation of her spiritual diary, which has become an overnight classic). John Paul suffered in many ways, made his ultimate sacrifice that now, as a Blessed, we know was received by the Blessed Mother – he, who was so devoted to Her - and his successor, our Pope Benedict XVI, will likely pass on to his eternal reward before we see "the triumph of the Church of God."

Also in this message, not unlike the others, Mary holds out the promise of a glorious reign of Christ: "The righteous will suffer greatly. Their prayers, their penance and their tears will rise up to Heaven and all of God's people will beg for forgiveness and mercy and will plead for My help and intercession. And then Jesus Christ, in an act of His justice and His great mercy will command His angels to have all His enemies put to death. Suddenly, the persecutors of the Church of Jesus Christ and all those given over to sin will perish and the earth will become desert-like. And then peace will be made, and man will be reconciled with God. Jesus Christ will be served, worshipped, and glorified. Charity will flourish everywhere. The new kings will be the right arm of the Holy Church, which will be strong, humble, pious in its poor but fervent in the imitation of the virtues of Jesus Christ. The Gospel will be preached everywhere and mankind will make great progress in its Faith, for there will be unity among the workers of Jesus Christ and man will live in fear of God." This seems to be the "new springtime" spoken of by John Paul and others, but interestingly, in this message, the Blessed Mother goes a step further by taking about what seems to be the era after the era of peace – specifically, the time of the Final Judgment, with the rise of the very person of the Antichrist. I will, however, withhold my sentiments on that particular topic, as the Final Judgment is beyond the scope of this book.

3. THE FIFTH AND FINAL MARIAN DOGMA

The significant, Church-approved Marian prophecies of Our Lady of All Nations in Amsterdam state that in the near future, on May 31, feast of Mary, Mediatrix of all Graces, a pope will solemnly declare the fifth and final Marian dogma in the Church's history; that of Mary's three-fold function as "Coredemptrix, Mediatrix and Advocate" for the People of God. The proclamation of this dogma is of tremendous significance, as it will result in a tremendous, unprecedented outpouring of the Holy Spirit upon humanity which will first take the form of a warning that will ultimately lead to the conversion of many, many souls. This world-wide warning, or illumination of conscience, will constitute one of the greatest and final acts of Mercy of God for the benefit of humanity, as it will result in mass conversions to the true faith. Second, this unleashing of the Holy Spirit upon humanity and the world will result in a new springtime of grace, holiness, justice and peace. The Church, too, will be utterly purified; it will be truly poor, chaste and humble, in imitation of its spotless Mother, Mary.

I encourage you to be a small part of Marian history by signing the petition located in the appendix of this book. It consists of an eloquently written letter to His Holiness, Pope Benedict XVI, humbly requesting, as a member of the baptized faithful, that the Holy Father solemnly declare the fifth Marian dogma of Mary as "Co-Redemptrix, Mediatrix and Advocate" for the People of God. Dr. Mark Miravalle, professor of Theology and Mariology at Franciscan University of Steubenville, has spearheaded the Vox Populi movement, which is a global petition drive to have Mary dogmatically defined under her three-fold function. He was able to secure over 7,000,000 signatures that were submitted to Blessed John Paul II, and is now re-igniting the movement under the pontificate of Benedict XVI.

The apparitions of Our Lady of All Nations have had their up's and down's in terms of Church recognition and approbation. Some remain confused regarding what the Church's most recent position on this series of apparitions is. For clarity's sake, I shall here reproduce a copy of an official Church document in which the bishop unequivocally states, "I have come to the conclusion that the apparitions of the Lady of All Nations in Amsterdam consist of a supernatural origin." This letter, by Jozef Marianus Punt, Bishop of Haarlem, which states his approval of the cult of devotion to Our Lady of All Nations, along with a statement of the theological accuracy of the content of the messages, is here reproduced in its entirety:

"May 31, 2002 - In Response to Inquiries Concerning the Lady of All Nations Apparitions"

"As Bishop of Haarlem/Amsterdam, I have been requested to make a statement regarding the authenticity of the apparitions of Mary as the Lady of All Nations in Amsterdam during the years of 1945 -1959. Many members of the faithful and bishops have emphasized the urgency for clarification. I also have been personally aware that this development of devotion, which has spanned over 50 years, call for this" (www.ewtn.com/expert/answers/OLAN2002.pdf).

"As it is known, my predecessor, Msgr. H. Bomers and myself had previously given permission for public veneration in 1996. As to the supernatural character of the apparitions and contents of the messages, we did not give our judgment, but declared that "everyone is free to make a judgment for himself or herself according to their conscience." Having had a generally positive attitude towards authenticity, we decided to await further development and to "discern the spirit" further (cf. 1 *Thes* 5:19-21)" (*ibid.*).

"Over the period of six subsequent years, I observed that the devotion had taken its place in the spiritual life of millions all over the world, and that it possesses the support of many bishops. Many experiences of conversion and reconciliation, as well as healings and special protection also have been reported to me. In full recognition of the responsibility of the Holy See, it is primarily the task of the local bishop to speak out in conscience regarding the authenticity of private revelations that take place or have taken place within his diocese. Therefore I have asked once again for the advice of theologians and psychologists concerning outcomes of previous investigations, and the questions and objections deriving from them. Their recommendations state that no theological or psychological impediments for a declaration of supernatural authenticity can be found therein. I have also requested the judgment of a number of brother bishops concerning the fruits and development of the devotion, who within their own dioceses have experienced a strong devotion of Mary as the Mother and Lady of All Nations. In light and virtue of all these recommendations, testimonies, and developments, and in pondering all this in prayer and theological reflection, I have come to the conclusion that the apparitions of the Lady of All Nations in Amsterdam consist of a supernatural origin" (*ibid.*).

"Naturally, the influence of the human element still exists. Authentic images and visions are always transmitted to us, in the words of Joseph Cardinal Ratzinger, Prefect of the Congregation of the Doctrine of Faith, "through the filter of our senses, which carry out a work of translation..." and "...are influenced by the potentialities and limitations of the perceiving subject" (Cardinal Ratzinger, *Theological Commentary In Preparation for the Release of the Third Part of the Secret of Fatima, L 'Osservatore Romano, June 28, 2000)" (ibid.)*.

"Unlike Holy Scripture, private revelations are never binding upon the conscience of the faithful. They are a help in understanding the signs of the times and to help live more fully the Gospel (cf. *Lk* 12:56, *Catechism of the Catholic Church, n. 67)*. And the signs of our times are dramatic. The devotion to the Lady of All Nations can help us, in my sincere conviction, in guiding us on the right path during the present serious drama of our times, the path to a new and special outpouring of the Holy Spirit, Who alone can heal the great wounds of our times" *(ibid.)*.

"To follow the further development of this devotion and to come to an even deeper insight into its meaning, I have installed a commission whose task it will be to continue to document all initiatives, experiences, and testimonies stemming from the devotion in order to help insure and preserve a correct ecclesial and theological progress of devotion. I hope this has provided sufficient information and clarification. Jozef Marianus Punt, Bishop of Haarlem" *(ibid.)*.

The Prophetic Messages of Our Lady of All Nations Regarding the Fifth Marian Dogma

What follows is a collection of some of the more salient messages concerning the future, final Marian dogma of Mary as Advocate, Co-Redemptrix and Mediatrix:

"Now I will explain something to you again; listen carefully. Try to understand what this message means. I am standing before the Cross with my head, hands and feet as of a human being; my body as of the Spirit. Why am I like this? My body has been taken up, like the Son. Now I am standing in sacrifice before the Cross. For I suffered with my Son spiritually and, above all, bodily. This will become a much contested "dogma" (www.circleofprayer.com/theladyofallnations.html).

"I say that this message makes me afraid. Then the Lady says, "Child, pass it on, and say: this brings the Marian dogmas to a close." While saying this, the Lady makes a kind of ring or circle, which, so to speak, she closes with a lock. You have nothing to do other than pass this on. Listen well and understand well what I am now going to explain. Once again I say: the Son came into the world as the Redeemer of humanity. The work of redemption was the Cross. He was sent by the Father. Now, however, the Father and the Son want to send the Lady throughout the whole world. For in the past, too, she went before the Son and followed Him. That is why I now stand on the world, on the globe. The Cross is firmly fixed upon it, implanted in it. Now the Lady places herself before it, as the Mother of the Son, who with Him accomplished this work of redemption. This image speaks for itself and shall already be brought into the world, because the world needs the Cross again" (*ibid.*).

"The Lady, however, stands as the Coredemptrix and Advocate before the Cross. Much controversy will arise over this. The Church, Rome, however, shall not be afraid to take up this struggle. It can only make the Church stronger and more powerful. This I am saying to theologians. Furthermore I tell them: take this matter seriously. Once again I say: the Son always looks for the little, the simple for His cause. Child, I hope you have grasped this well and can refute all objections" (*ibid.*).

"I stand here as the Co-Redemptrix and Advocate. Every thought should be directed at that. Repeat this after me: the new dogma shall be the dogma of the Coredemptrix. 'Co'—this I stress especially. I have said: much controversy will arise over that. Once again I tell you: the Church, Rome, will carry through with it and fight for it. The Church, Rome, will incur opposition and stand firm. The Church, Rome, will grow stronger and more powerful insofar as she stands firm in the fight. My intention and my instruction for you is none other than to urge the Church, the theologians, onward to this fight. For the Father, the Son, the Spirit want to bring the Lady, chosen to bring the Redeemer, into this world as Co-Redemptrix and Advocate" (*ibid.*).

"I stand here and come to tell you that I wish to be Mary, the Lady of All Nations. Look carefully. I am standing before the Cross of the Redeemer. My head, hands and feet as of a human being, as of the Son of Man; the body as of the Spirit. I have firmly placed my feet upon the globe, for in this time the Father and the Son want to bring me into this world as Coredemptrix, Mediatrix and Advocate. This will be the new and final Marian dogma. This image will precede. Now look carefully and listen. The following is an explanation of the new dogma. As Co-Redemptrix,

Mediatrix and Advocate, I stand on the globe before the Cross of the Redeemer. By the will of the Father, the Redeemer came to the world. For this, the Father used the Lady. Thus, from the Lady the Redeemer received only—now I am stressing the word 'only'—the flesh and blood, that is to say, the body. From my Lord and Master the Redeemer received His Divinity. In this way the Lady became the Co-Redemptrix" (*ibid.*).

"The Lady of All Nations stands in the middle of the world before the Cross. She comes under this name as the Co-Redemptrix, Mediatrix and Advocate, in this time. She will be taken up into Marian history under this title. The new and final dogma of Marian history will be the dogma of the Co-Redemptrix and Mediatrix. As Advocate I stand now in this anxious time. All of you, no matter who or what you are, ask that the true Holy Spirit may come. This you shall ask the Father and the Son. The Divine Trinity will again reign over the world. The Lady stands here as the Advocate. The issue here is the Creator, not the Lady. Tell this to your theologians. Ask them to send this simple prayer throughout the world and the Lady will give the strength and power to carry it through" (*ibid.*).

4. PROCLAMATION OF THE DOGMA

Proclamation Will Result in Great Outpouring of the Holy Spirit, a Worldwide Warning and Purification

Mary speaks extensively of the "Second Pentecost," the "Illumination," or, as some have referred to it, the "Warning." This tremendous grace and gift of God, as spoken of earlier, will be one of God's greatest acts of mercy in and for these times in which we live. According to various private revelations, it will be like a "judgment in miniature," by which all the living inhabitants of earth will see and understand the sinful state of their souls in the burning fire of God's light and truth. Sr. Lucy, the longest living of the Fatima visionaries, alluded to this illumination of conscience when she stated the following in the Third Secret: "And we saw in an immense light that is God: 'something similar to how people appear in a mirror when they pass in front of it.'"

The Blessed Mother provides a more detailed explanation of this illumination that is to come to Fr. Gobbi of the Marian Movement of Priests (MMP), in the book, *To the Priests, Our Lady's Beloved Sons*: "The Holy Spirit will come, to establish the glorious reign of Christ, and it will be a reign of grace, of holiness, of love, of justice and of peace. With His divine love, He will open the doors of hearts and illuminate all consciences. Every person will see himself in the burning fire of divine truth. It will be like a judgment in miniature. And then Jesus Christ will bring His glorious reign in the world" (Gobbi, 565, Message 383, Para. D).

What we need to understand is the intimate connection between the proclamation of the fifth and final Marian Dogma and this unleashing of the Holy Spirit in the form of a new, Second Pentecost. In essence, the Church, in defining as dogma the three-fold function of Mary as Coredemptrix, Mediatrix and Advocate, will place this truth at the very top of the "hierarchy of truths," along with the many other dogmatic truths taught and promulgated by the Church. It will be the final Marian dogma because it perfectly expresses 1. Mary's cooperation with Christ in the redemption of humanity – a co-operation that is entirely subordinate to and dependant on the perfect redemptive action of Christ, the sole mediator between the Father and humanity; 2. The reality that every grace that comes to humanity comes through the willed intercession of Mary; and 3. The role that Mary has as the great advocate and intercessor on behalf of humanity. These three functions of Mary best express her action as Spiritual Mother of the Mystical Body of Christ, the Church, and Mother of all of humanity.

The Church's official designation, recognition and proclamation of Mary's Spiritual Motherhood, specifically according to these three functions, and in the form of a dogmatic pronunciation, will constitute the definitive act that will enable Mary, the true spouse of the Holy Spirit, to obtain for the Church a new, super-abundant outpouring of the Holy Spirit in the form of a new, Second Pentecost. This Second Pentecost will truly transform the hearts of each individual and will renew the Church and the world, ushering in a new springtime of grace, holiness, peace and authentic ecumenical unity, with one flock and one shepherd. Dr. Mark Miravalle, contemporary Mariologist, explained to the Catholic news agency, Zenit, the following: "In light of the present world climate of war and rumours of war, I believe the proclamation of the dogma of Mary Co-redemptrix, Mediatrix of all graces and Advocate would be the means to release the full exercise of Our Lady's motherly intercessory role in bringing peace to a troubled world, in fulfilment of her Fatima promise that 'in the end my Immaculate Heart will triumph ... and a period of peace will be granted to the world.' God respects human freedom, and the papal proclamation would 'free her' to exercise fully her saving roles for contemporary humanity"
(www.fifthmariandogma.com/index.php?option=com_content&view=art icle&id=216:why-now-is-the-time-for-a-dogma-of-mary-co-redemptrix&catid=105:articles&Itemid=582).

Furthermore, La Salette Journey Blog has this to say: "Our Lady revealed to Ida Peerdeman during her fiftieth vision on May 31, 1954, that on a future date of May 31, the Co-Redemptrix, Mediatrix, and Advocate would receive her official title of Our Lady of All Nations. In the course of the same message, the Lady also said: 'When the dogma--the last dogma in Marian history--has been proclaimed, the Lady of All Nations would procure peace, genuine peace for the world. But the nations must say my prayer in union with the Church. Then they will experience that the Lady has come as Co-Redemptrix, Mediatrix, and Advocate. So be it.'"
(http://lasalettejourney.blogspot.com/2009/05/one-step-closer-to-fifth-marian-dogma.html)

Within the same post on La Salette Journey's Blog, the author states the following: "The Devil and his followers know that when Our Lady is proclaimed Co-Redemptrix, their end will soon be at hand. This fifth Marian Dogma is the key to the Triumph of the Immaculate Heart of

Mary and will lead to an outpouring of the Holy Spirit such as has not been seen since the first Pentecost. This Second Pentecost will signal total and decisive defeat for the Devil and his followers. Which is why the forces of ecclesiastical masonry have always and everywhere opposed this fifth Marian Dogma"

(http://lasalettejourney.blogspot.com/2009/05/one-step-closer-to-fifth-marian-dogma.html).

What is more, the Church teaches that Mary is the true "spouse" of the Holy Spirit. The Holy Spirit acts only with the consent of his spouse, the Blessed Virgin Mary. We must understand that God has freely chosen to work through Mary in this radical fashion, as will be explained at length in the second section of this book. God has chosen to involve Mary in an intimate fashion is His plan of salvation, particularly in these end times. Once the dogma is defined and proclaimed, the Holy Spirit, the spouse of Mary, who has chosen to be dependent on her Maternal Mediation, will come by means of the powerful intercession of the Immaculate Heart of Mary.

Speaking on the effects of the new, Second Pentecost, Mary states the following to Fr. Gobbi: "The Holy Spirit will come, as heavenly dew of grace and of fire, which will renew all the world. Under His irresistible action of love, the Church will open itself to live the new era of its greatest holiness and will shine resplendently with so strong a light that it will attract to itself all the nations of the earth. The Holy Spirit will come, that the will of the Heavenly Father be accomplished and the created universe once again reflect His great glory....The Holy Spirit will come, by means of the Triumph of My Immaculate Heart. For this, I am calling upon you all today to enter into the cenacle of My Heart. Thus, you will be prepared to receive the gift of the Holy Spirit which will transform you and make you the instruments with which Jesus will establish His reign" (Gobbi, 565, Message 383, Para. B-E).

Thus, the proclamation of the Marian dogma is the key that will unlock the door of an unprecedented outpouring of the Holy Spirit, the likes of which the world has never before witnessed, and this will both coincide with the Triumph of Mary's Immaculate Heart, foretold at Fatima, and prepare the world for the glorious reign of Christ.

Patron Saint of Our Difficult Century,
St. Maximilian Kolbe

A truly great Marian saint, canonized by Blessed John Paul II and proclaimed the "Patron of Our Difficult Century" – that is, the twentieth century - is St. Maximilian Kolbe. Kolbe foresaw the tremendous role that total consecration to Mary would play in the end times – our times. Canonized on October 10, 1982, he was declared to be a martyr of charity for having taken the place of another concentration camp victim who was chosen to die a slow, excruciating death in a starvation bunker. Throughout his imprisonment, he worked to keep up the spirits of the other prisoners by singing Marian hymns and using the meager rations to clandestinely celebrate Holy Mass. At the end, after multiple days in the starvation bunker, and being the only remaining survivor, the Nazi's decided to kill him via lethal injection on August 14, the vigil of the great Marian Solemnity of the Assumption. It is because of this fact that he is recognized as the patron saint of the chemically addicted. And due to his being a prisoner of conscience, he is likewise the patron of political prisoners. Finally, he is invoked by many as the patron saint of families, journalists, prisoners in general, and the pro-life movement.

It was no coincidence that he entered into his eternal reward on the vigil of a great Marian Feast, considering his tremendous devotion to the Blessed Virgin. He wrote extensively on the radical importance of consecration to Mary, prophetically viewing this devotion as necessary for the protection, sanctification and salvation of souls. In fact, it was shortly after a vehemently anti-Catholic demonstration in St. Peter's Square put on by the Freemasons that Kolbe decided to found the Militia Immaculata, a spiritual society/organization, and eventually Marytown, a place where the Coventual Franciscans could live, work and pray together in a spirit of filial dependence on the Blessed Virgin Mary. Of the Militia Immaculata (MI), Kolbe has stated, "That which constitutes the essence of every society, or that which unites the members in tending toward the end, is its form. In the MI the form is the entire and unrestricted dedication to the Immaculate Virgin Mary, so that she might deign to perform in and through us what has been written of her, 'She will crush thy head' and 'Thou alone has destroyed all heresies in the whole world.'

"The spirit is what vivifies and urges us on. The spirit of the MI will give life to its members, so that they may be Knights of the Immaculata more and more, and so that they may daily become more and more the property and possession of the Immaculata, and more zealously win for her the hearts of their neighbors. The more they are imbued with this spirit, the greater Knights of the Immaculata they will be. The motto of the Militia Immaculata is 'To lead all men and every individual through Mary to the most Sacred Heart of Jesus.' In other words, the Immaculata must become the queen of each and every soul" (Kolbe, 44-45). And St. Kolbe spent himself entirely for this purpose, to the point of heroically laying down his own life for that of a brother in Christ.

It is no coincidence that this apostle of Mary, whose entire mission in life was to have as many souls as possible consecrate themselves to Mary, was named the "Patron of Our Difficult Century" – the Twentieth Century – which is under the dominion of Satan. This only serves to underscore the truth that Marian consecration is, indeed, the antidote to the spiritually infectious disease of Marxist Atheism, and serves as a shield protecting Mary's clients from the seductions of the Evil One.

5. PROPHETIC INTERPRETATION OF CHAPTERS 12-13 OF THE BOOK OF REVELATION

In messages 403-407 in the book *To the Priests, Our Lady's Beloved Sons*, Our Lady reveals to Fr. Gobbi the hidden meaning behind the prophecies contained in the 12th and 13th Chapters of St. John's Book of Revelation. These messages are of profound importance and unveil and decode the true meaning of the above mentioned apocalyptic verses. For the sake of organization and continuity, Chapters 12 and 13 of the Book of Revelation will be reproduced below in their entirety, to be followed by a prophetic exegesis of the true meaning of the highly symbolic content of these most mysterious passages in all of Scripture.

Revelation, Chapter 12

"And a great sign appeared in heaven: A woman clothed with the sun, and the moon under her feet, and on her head a crown of twelve stars: And being with child, she cried travailing in birth, and was in pain to be delivered. And there was seen another sign in heaven: and behold a great red dragon, having seven heads, and ten horns: and on his head seven diadems: And his tail drew the third part of the stars of heaven, and cast them to the earth: and the dragon stood before the woman who was ready to be delivered; that, when she should be delivered, he might devour her son. And she brought forth a man child, who was to rule all nations with an iron rod: and her son was taken up to God, and to his throne."

"And the woman fled into the wilderness, where she had a place prepared by God, that there they should feed her a thousand two hundred sixty days. And there was a great battle in heaven, Michael and his angels fought with the dragon, and the dragon fought and his angels: And they prevailed not, neither was their place found any more in heaven. And that great dragon was cast out, that old serpent, who is called the devil and Satan, who seduceth the whole world; and he was cast unto the earth, and his angels were thrown down with him. And I heard a loud voice in heaven, saying: Now is come salvation, and strength, and the kingdom of our God, and the power of his Christ: because the accuser of our brethren is cast forth, who accused them before our God day and night."

"And they overcame him by the blood of the Lamb, and by the word of the testimony, and they loved not their lives unto death. Therefore rejoice, O heavens, and you that dwell therein. Woe to the earth, and to the sea, because the devil is come down unto you, having great wrath, knowing that he hath but a short time. And when the dragon saw that he was cast unto the earth, he persecuted the woman, who brought forth the man child: And there were given to the woman two wings of a great eagle, that she might fly into the desert unto her place, where she is nourished for a time and times, and half a time, from the face of the serpent. And the serpent cast out of his mouth after the woman, water as it were a river; that he might cause her to be carried away by the river."

"And the earth helped the woman, and the earth opened her mouth, and swallowed up the river, which the dragon cast out of his mouth. And the dragon was angry against the woman: and went to make war with the rest of her seed, who keep the commandments of God, and have the testimony of Jesus Christ. And he stood upon the sand of the sea."

Revelation, Chapter 13

"And I saw a beast coming up out of the sea, having seven heads and ten horns, and upon his horns ten diadems, and upon his heads names of blasphemy. And the beast, which I saw, was like to a leopard, and his feet were as the feet of a bear, and his mouth as the mouth of a lion. And the dragon gave him his own strength, and great power. And I saw one of his heads as it were slain to death: and his death wound was healed. And all the earth was in admiration after the beast. And they adored the dragon, which gave power to the beast: and they adored the beast, saying: Who is like to the beast? and who shall be able to fight with him? And there was given to him a mouth speaking great things, and blasphemies: and power was given to him to do two and forty months."

"And he opened his mouth unto blasphemies against God, to blaspheme his name, and his tabernacle, and them that dwell in heaven. And it was given unto him to make war with the saints, and to overcome them. And power was given him over every tribe, and people, and tongue, and nation. And all that dwell upon the earth adored him, whose names are not written in the book of life of the Lamb, which was slain from the beginning of the world. If any man have an ear, let him hear. He that shall lead into captivity, shall go into captivity: he that shall kill by the sword, must be killed by the sword. Here is the patience and the faith of the saints."

"And I saw another beast coming up out of the earth, and he had two horns, like a lamb, and he spoke as a dragon. And he executed all the power of the former beast in his sight; and he caused the earth, and them that dwell therein, to adore the first beast, whose wound to death was healed. And he did great signs, so that he made also fire to come down from heaven unto the earth in the sight of men. And he seduced them that dwell on the earth, for the signs, which were given him to do in the sight of the beast, saying to them that dwell on the earth, that they should make the image of the beast, which had the wound by the sword, and lived. And it was given him to give life to the image of the beast, and that the image of the beast should speak; and should cause, that whosoever will not adore the image of the beast, should be slain."

"And he shall make all, both little and great, rich and poor, freemen and bondmen, to have a character in their right hand, or on their foreheads. And that no man might buy or sell, but he that hath the character, or the name of the beast, or the number of his name. Here is wisdom. He that hath understanding, let him count the number of the beast. For it is the number of a man: and the number of him is six hundred sixty-six" (www.drbo.org/chapter/73012.htm).

Exegetical Interpretation Using the Interior Locutions of Mary to Fr. Gobbi

The "Woman clothed with the sun, with the moon under her feet, and on her head, a crown of twelve stars," clearly represents the Blessed Mother. She is bathed in the divine light of Christ, which explains her being "clothed with the sun." The moon is symbolic in that the actual moon can only be seen by humans on earth because it is reflecting the light of the sun. Mary is the purest reflection of the light of Christ, the Son and the Sun. The crown of twelve stars is symbolic of three things: first, it represents the 12 Tribes of Israel, Gods Chosen People; second, it represents the 12 apostles, the foundation of the Church of Christ, who went on to replace the 12 Tribes when Christ established the new and everlasting covenant between God and all humanity in His blood; third, the crown is representative of all the children of Mary, spoken of in Genesis 3:15 – Mary's offspring – the first of whom is Christ. All of Mary's "victim-souls," all those little ones totally consecrated to her, whose prayer and suffering are being offered by Mary to the Heavenly Father to appease His just wrath, make up her crown of glory. Thus, the "heel" of the mystical body is likewise and necessarily the crown of Mary – the smallest on earth are the greatest in the Kingdom of Heaven.

Now there is a cosmic battle taking place between the "Woman clothed with the Sun" and "a great Red Dragon, having seven heads, and ten horns." In message 404 of *To the Priests...* Mary states the following: "The huge Red Dragon is atheistic communism which has spread everywhere the error of the denial and of the obstinate rejection of God. The huge Red Dragon is Marxist atheism, which appears with ten horns, namely with the power of its means of communication, in order to lead humanity to disobey the ten commandments of God, and with seven heads, upon each of which there is a crown, signs of authority and royalty. The crowned heads indicate the nations in which atheistic communism is established and rules with the force of its ideological, political and military power. The hugeness of the Dragon clearly manifests the vastness of the territory occupied by the uncontested reign of atheistic communism. Its color is red because it uses wars and blood as instruments of its numerous conquests" (Gobbi, 599-600, Message 404, Para. E-H).

"The huge Red Dragon has succeeded during these years in conquering humanity with the error of theoretical and practical atheism, which has now seduced all the nations of the earth. It has thus succeeded in building up for itself a new civilization without God, materialistic, egoistic, hedonistic, arid and cold, which carries within itself the seeds of corruption and death. The huge Red Dragon has the diabolical task of taking all humanity away from the dominion of God, from the glorification of the Most Holy Trinity, from the full actualization of the plan of the Father who, by means of the Son, has created it for His Glory" (*ibid.*).

Shortly after Mary is proclaimed as the "Woman clothed with the sun" who enters into a cosmic battle with the "huge Red Dragon," it is stated that the Dragon's "tail drew the third part of the stars of heaven, and cast them to the earth." In message 99 of *To the Priests...* Mary states, "Now you are living in that period of time when the Red Dragon, that is to say Marxist Atheism, is spreading throughout the world and is increasingly bringing about the ruin of souls. He is indeed succeeding in seducing and casting down a third of the starts in heaven. These stars, in the firmament of the Church, are the Pastors: they are yourselves, my poor priest-sons."

Revelation 12:7-10 speaks about the cosmic battle taking place throughout the course of human history, and how St. Michael's victory over Satan has already been foretold: "And there was a great battle in heaven, Michael and his angels fought with the dragon, and the dragon fought and his angels: And they prevailed not, neither was their place found any more in heaven. And that great dragon was cast out, that old serpent, who is called the devil and Satan, who seduceth the whole world; and he was cast unto the earth, and his angels were thrown down with him. And I heard a loud voice in heaven, saying: Now is come salvation, and strength, and the kingdom of our God, and the power of his Christ: because the accuser of our brethren is cast forth, who accused them before our God day and night."

In Revelation 12:12-15, we read, "Woe to the earth, and to the sea, because the devil is come down unto you, having great wrath, knowing that he hath but a short time. And when the dragon saw that he was cast unto the earth, he persecuted the woman, who brought forth the man child: And there were given to the woman two wings of a great eagle, that she might fly into the desert unto her place, where she is nourished for a time and times, and half a time, from the face of the serpent. And the serpent cast out of his mouth after the woman, water as it were a river; that he might cause her to be carried away by the river." This section refers to the "latter-day," the "end-times" through which we are now living. A distinction should be made between the term, the "latter-times," used broadly by theologians to refer to the entire period of history following Christ's incarnation, life, passion, death and resurrection, and the same term used to refer to the end of the end, as it were, or the end-times of the broader "latter-days." The end-times of which we speak refer to this latter sense, the end of the end, or the apex of the cosmic battle between the "Woman clothed with the Sun" and the "huge Red dragon."

In the passages that follow, the ancient serpent, who is the devil or Satan, has been cast out of heaven and has been sent to the earth to seduce its inhabitants and to steal as many souls away from God for himself. Yet he knows his time is short. Meanwhile, Mary is given the two wings of a great eagle, that she might fly above the torrent of water that Satan has spewed at her, and take refuge into a place prepared for her in the desert. Mary explains the meaning of this symbolism to Fr. Gobbi:

"But to the help of your heavenly Mother, there have come the two wings of the great eagle. The great eagle is the word of God, above all the word contained in the Gospel of my Son, Jesus. Of the four Gospels, the eagle indicates that of Saint John, because he flies higher than all, enters into the very heart of the Most Holy Trinity, affirming with forcefulness the divinity, the eternity and the consubstantiality of the Word and the divinity of Jesus Christ. The two wings of the eagle are the word of God, received, loved and kept with *faith* and the word of God *lived* with *grace* and *charity*. The two wings of faith and charity – that is to say, of the word of God received and lived by me – permitted me to fly above the river of water of all the attacks made upon me, because they have manifested to the world my true greatness. And then I sought a refuge for myself in the desert. The desert, in which I have made my habitual dwelling place, is made up of the hearts and the souls of all those children who receive me, who listen to me, who entrust themselves completely to me, who consecrate themselves to my Immaculate Heart. In the desert in which I find myself, I am working today my greatest prodigies. I am working them in the heart and in the soul, that is to say, in the life of all my littlest children. Thus I am leading them to follow me along the road of faith and of charity, bringing them to receive, to love and to keep the Word of God and helping them to live each day with consistency and courage" (Gobbi, 597-98, Message 403, Para. G).

In Rev.13:1-2, we read the following: "And I saw a beast coming up out of the sea, having seven heads and ten horns, and upon his horns ten diadems, and upon his heads names of blasphemy. And the beast, which I saw, was like to a leopard, and his feet were as the feet of a bear, and his mouth as the mouth of a lion. And the dragon gave him his own strength, and great power." Speaking on this, Mary explains to Fr. Gobbi the following: "In this terrible struggle, there comes up from the sea, to the aid of the Dragon, a beast like a leopard. If the Red Dragon is Marxist atheism, the Black Beast is Freemasonry. The Dragon manifests himself in the force of his power; the Black Beast, on the other hand, acts in the shadow, keeps out of sight and hides himself in such a way as to enter into everywhere. He has the claws of a bear and the mouth of a lion, because he works everywhere with cunning and with the means of social communication, that is to say, through propaganda. The seven heads indicate the various Masonic lodges, which act everywhere in a subtle and dangerous way"

"This Black Beast has ten horns and, on the horns, ten crowns, which are signs of dominion and royalty. Masonry rules and governs throughout the whole world by means of the ten horns. The horn, in the biblical world, has always been an instrument of amplification, a way of making one's voice better heard, a strong means of communication. For this reason, God communicated His will to His people by means of ten horns which made His law known: the Ten Commandments. The one who accepts them and observes them walks in life along the road of the Divine Will, of joy, and of peace. The one who does the Will of the Father accepts the word of His Son and shares in the redemption accomplished by Him. Jesus gives to souls the very divine life, through grace, that He won for us through His sacrifice carried out on Calvary. The grace of the redemption is communicated by means of the seven sacraments. With grace there becomes implanted in the soul the seeds of supernatural life which are the virtues. Among these, the most important are the three theological and the four cardinal virtues: faith, hope, charity; prudence, fortitude, justice and temperance. In the divine sun of the seven gifts of the Holy Spirit, these virtues germinate, grow, become more and more developed and thus lead the soul along the luminous way of love and sanctity."

"The task of the Black Beast, namely of Masonry, is that of fighting, in a subtle way, but tenaciously, to obstruct souls from traveling along this way, pointed out by the Father and the Son and lighted up by the gifts of the Holy Spirit. In fact if the Red Dragon works to bring all humanity to do without God, to the denial of God, and therefore spreads the error of atheism, the aim of Masonry is not to deny God, but to blaspheme Him. The Beast opens his mouth to utter blasphemies against God, to blaspheme His name and His dwelling place, and against all those who dwell in heaven. The greatest blasphemy is that of denying the worship due to God alone by giving it to creatures and to Satan himself. This is why in these times, behind the perverse action of Freemasonry, there are being spread everywhere black masses and the satanic cult. Moreover Masonry acts, by every means, to prevent souls from being saved, and thus it endeavors to bring to nothing the redemption accomplished by Christ."

The message continues on to explain how Freemasonry systematically promotes ways of living, acting and behaving that are diametrically opposed to the Ten Commandments of God. In opposition to the first commandment, it sets up all sorts of false idols to adore; it opposes the second commandment by promoting the blasphemous use of God's name in films, television, to promote products, and so on; it opposes the third commandment by transforming Sunday into "the weekend," a time to watch sports and engage in every sort of entertainment to the exclusion of God; it opposes the fourth commandment by promoting new, updated, "politically-correct" models of the family based on cohabitation, homosexual domestic partnership and even marriage, allowing homosexual couples to adopt and raise children, and so on; it opposes the fifth commandment by making abortion and euthanasia legal everywhere, and promoting the "culture of death;" it opposes the commandments that prohibit impurity by promoting every form of deviant sexual behavior, even sins against nature; in opposition the commandment, "You shall not steal," it promotes violence, kidnapping and robbery; in opposition to the commandment "You shall not bear false witness," it promotes lying, duplicity, and deceit; in opposition to the commandment, "You shall not covet the goods and the wife of another," it promotes the death of the conscience such that anything and everything is up for grabs and for the taking. What is more, freemasonry counters the three theological virtues of faith, hope and charity with pride, lust and avarice respectively. It counters the four cardinal virtues of prudence, justice, fortitude and temperance with anger, envy, sloth, and gluttony respectively.

Further on, in Rev. 13:11-12, we read, "And I saw another beast coming up out of the earth, and he had two horns, like a lamb, and he spoke as a dragon. And he executed all the power of the former beast in his sight; and he caused the earth, and them that dwell therein, to adore the first beast..." In message 406 of *To the Priest...*, Our Lady states the following: "...there comes out of the earth, by way of aid to the Black Beast which arises out of the sea, a beast which has two horns like those of a lamb. The lamb, in Holy Scripture, has always been a symbol of sacrifice. On the night of the exodus, the lamb is sacrificed, and, with its blood, the doorposts of the houses of the Hebrews are sprinkled, in order to remove them from the punishment which on the contrary strikes all the Egyptians. The Hebrew Pasch recalls this fact each year, through the immolation of a lamb, which is sacrificed and consumed. On Calvary, Jesus Christ sacrifices Himself for the redemption of humanity; He Himself becomes our Pasch and becomes the true Lamb of God who takes away all the sins of the world."

"The beast has on its head two horns like those of a lamb. To the symbol of sacrifice, there is intimately connected that of the priesthood: the two horns. The high priest of the Old Testament wore a headpiece with two horns. The bishops of the Church wear a miter with two horns to indicate the fullness of their priesthood. The black beast like a leopard indicates Freemasonry; the beast with the two horns like a lamb indicates Freemasonry infiltrated into the interior of the Church, that is to say, ecclesiastical Masonry, which has spread especially among the members of the hierarchy. This Masonic infiltration, in the interior of the Church, was already foretold to you by me at Fatima, when I announced to you that Satan would enter in even to the summit of the Church. If the task of Masonry is to lead souls to perdition, bringing them to the worship of false divinities, the task of ecclesiastical Masonry on the other hand is that of destroying Christ and His Church, building a new idol, namely a false christ and a false church."

"Jesus Christ is the Son of the living God; He is the Word incarnate; He is true God and true Man because He unites in His divine Person human nature and divine nature. Jesus, in the Gospel, has given His most complete definition of Himself, saying that He is the Truth, the Way and the Life. Jesus is the Truth, because He reveals the Father to us, speaks His definitive word to us, and brings all divine revelation to its perfect fulfillment. Jesus is the Life, because He gives us divine life itself, with the grace merited by Him through redemption, and He institutes the sacraments as efficacious means which communicate grace. Jesus is the Way which leads to the Father, by means of the Gospel which He has given us, as the way to follow to attain salvation. Jesus is the Truth because it is He – the living Word – who is the font and seal of all divine revelation. And so ecclesiastical Masonry works to obscure his divine word, by means of natural and rational interpretations and, in the attempt to make it more understandable and acceptable, empties it of all its supernatural content. Thus, errors are spread in every part of the Catholic Church itself. Because of the spread of these errors, many are moving away today from the true faith, bringing to fulfillment the prophecy which was given to you by me at Fatima: 'The times will come when many will lose the true faith.' The loss of the faith is apostasy. Ecclesiastical Masonry works, in a subtle and diabolical way, to lead all into apostasy."

"Jesus is the Life because He gives grace. The aim of ecclesiastical Masonry is that of justifying sin, of presenting it no longer as an evil but as something good and of value. Thus one is advised to do this as a way of satisfying the exigencies of one's own nature, destroying the root from which repentance could be born, and is told that it is no longer necessary to confess it. The pernicious fruit of this accursed cancer, which has spread throughout the whole Church, is the disappearance everywhere of individual confession. Souls are led to live in sin, rejecting the gift of life which Jesus has offered us. Jesus is the Way which leads to the Father, by means of the Gospel. Ecclesiastical Masonry favors those forms of exegesis which give it a rationalistic and natural interpretation, by means of the application of various literary genres, in such a way that it becomes torn to pieces in all its parts. In the end, one arrives at denying the historical reality of miracles and of the resurrection and places in doubt the very divinity of Jesus and His salvific mission."

"After having destroyed the historical Christ, the beast with the two horns like a lamb seeks to destroy the mystical Christ which is the Church. The Church instituted by Christ is one, and one alone: it is the one, holy, catholic and apostolic Church, founded on Peter. As is Jesus, so too is the Church founded by Him which forms his Mystical Body, truth, life and way. The Church is truth, because Jesus has entrusted to it alone the task of guarding, in its integrity, all the deposit of faith. He has entrusted it to the hierarchical Church, that is to say, to the Pope and to the bishops united with him. Ecclesiastical Masonry seeks to destroy this reality through false ecumenism, which leads to the acceptance of all Christian Churches, asserting that each one of them has some part of the truth. It develops the plan of founding a universal ecumenical Church, formed by the fusion of all the Christian confessions, among which, the Catholic Church."

"The Church is life because it gives grace, and it alone possesses the efficacious means of grace, which are the seven sacraments. Especially it is life because to it alone is given the power to beget the Eucharist, by means of the hierarchical and ministerial priesthood. In the Eucharist, Jesus Christ is truly present with his glorified Body and his Divinity. And so ecclesiastical Masonry, in many and subtle ways, seeks to attack the ecclesial devotion towards the sacrament of the Eucharist. It gives value only to the meal aspect, tends to minimize its sacrificial value, seeks to deny the real and personal presence of Jesus in the consecrated Host. In this way there are gradually suppressed all the external signs which are indicative of faith in the real presence of Jesus in the Eucharist, such as genuflections, hours of public adoration and the holy custom of surrounding the tabernacle with lights and flowers."

"The Church is the way because it leads to the Father, through the Son, in the Holy Spirit, along the way of perfect unity. As the Father and the Son are one, so too must you be one among yourselves. Jesus has willed that His Church be a sign and an instrument of the unity of the whole human race. The Church succeeds in being united because it has been founded on the cornerstone of its unity: Peter, and the Pope who succeeds to the charism of Peter. And so ecclesiastical Masonry seeks to destroy the foundation of the unity of the Church, through a subtle and insidious attack on the Pope. It weaves plots of dissension and of contestation against the Pope; it supports and rewards those who vilify and disobey him; it disseminates the criticisms and the contentions of bishops and theologians. In this way the very foundation of its unity is demolished and thus the Church becomes more and more torn and divided" (Gobbi, Message 406).

The Blog, La Salette Journey, contains an article that sheds light on ecclesiastical Freemasonry. What follows is an excerpt from the end of the article that explains just how the false church shall be established: "We have witnessed the gradual emergence of this false church within Christ's Church. And that which this false church proposes is a new religion in which man, and not God, is the object of worship. And all will be accomplished in the name of humanitarianism. Through one of his characters in his prophetic book *The Lord of the World*, Fr. Robert Hugh Benson describes this humanitarian religion:"

"'Humanitarianism…is becoming an actual religion itself, though anti-supernatural. It is pantheism. Pantheism deifies all nature, God is the world, but naturally, man above all is God since he is the highest expression of nature. It is a religion devoid of the 'super' natural, because since God is nature itself, there is no longer a distinction between Creator and creature. The creature is God and hence arbitrator of his own destiny and establishes the moral law for himself. Nature, and man is its highest expression, has all the divine attributes. Humanitarianism is a religion devoid of the supernatural. It is developing a ritual under Freemasonry; it has a creed, 'God is man'; and the rest. It has, therefore, a real food of a sort to offer religious cravings: it idealizes, and yet makes no demands upon the spiritual faculties. Then, they have the use of all the churches except ours, and of all the Cathedrals; and they are beginning at last to encourage sentiment. Then they may display their symbols and we may not: I think they will be established legally in another ten years'" (http://lasalettejourney.blogspot.com/2007/03/ecclesiastical-freemasonry-and-religion.html).

The messages thus far have provided profound insights into the symbolic meaning of Chapters 12 and 13, pivotal chapters, of St. John's Book of Revelation. Before we finish this section, however, let us explore what the Blessed Mother has to say about the final lines of Chapter 13 of the Book of Revelation, which speak of the name and number of the beast as 666. Much ink has been spilled on the meaning of this satanic number, but, thanks to Our Lady's profound messages to Fr. Gobbi, we can finally understand its true meaning. Chapter 13 of the Book of Revelation ends with the following statement: "He that hath understanding, let him count the number of the beast. For it is the number of a man: and the number of him is six hundred sixty-six." Here is what the Blessed Mother has to say about the significance of this satanic name and number: "In the thirteenth chapter of the Apocalypse, it is written, 'This calls for wisdom. Let him who has understanding recon the number of the beast: it represents a human name. And the number in question is 666.'(Rev. 13:18). With intelligence, enlightened by the light of divine wisdom, one can succeed in deciphering from the number, 666, the name of a man and this name, indicated by such a number, is that of the Antichrist."

"Lucifer, the ancient serpent, the devil or Satan, the Red Dragon, becomes, in these last times, the Antichrist. The Apostle John already affirmed that whoever denies that Jesus Christ is God, that person is the

Antichrist. The statue or idol, built in honor of the Beast to be adored by all men, is the Antichrist. Calculate now its number, 666, to understand how it indicates the name of a man. The number, 333, indicates the divinity. Lucifer rebels against God through pride, because he wants to put himself above God. 333 is the number which indicates the mystery of God. He who wants to put himself above God bears the sign, 666, and consequently this number indicates the name of Lucifer, Satan, that is to say, of him who sets himself against Christ, of the Antichrist."

"333 indicated once, that is to say, for the first time, expresses the mystery of the unity of God. 333 indicated twice, that is to say, for the second time, indicates the two natures, that of the divine and the human, united in the Divine Person of Jesus Christ. 333 indicated thrice, that is to say, for the third time, indicates the mystery of Three Divine Persons, that is to say, it expresses the mystery of the Most Holy Trinity. Thus the number, 333, expressed one, two and three times, expresses the principal mysteries of the Catholic faith, which are: (1) the Unity and the Trinity of God, (2) the incarnation, the passion and death, and the resurrection of Our Lord Jesus Christ."

"If 333 is the number which indicates the divinity, he who wants to put himself above God Himself is referred to by the number 666. 666 indicated once, that is to say, for the first time, expresses the year 666, six hundred and sixty-six. In this period of history, the Antichrist is manifested through the phenomenon of Islam, which directly denies the mystery of the Divine Trinity and the Divinity of Our Lord Jesus Christ. Islamism, with its military force, breaks loose everywhere, destroying all the ancient Christian communities, and invades Europe, and it is only through my extraordinary motherly intervention, begged for powerfully by the Holy Father, that it does not succeed in destroying Christianity completely. 666 indicated twice, that is to say, for the second time, expresses the year 1332, thirteen hundred and thirty-two. In this period of history, the Antichrist is manifested through a radical attack on the faith in the word of God. Through the philosophers who begin to give exclusive value to science and then to reason, there is a gradual tendency to constitute human intelligence alone as the sole criterion of truth. There comes to birth the great philosophical errors which continue through the centuries down to your days. The exaggerated importance given to reason, as an exclusive criterion of truth, necessarily leads to the destruction of the faith in the word of God. Indeed, with the Protestant Reformation, Tradition is rejected as a source of divine revelation, and only Sacred Scripture is accepted. But even this must be interpreted by means of the reason, and the authentic Magisterium of the hierarchical Church, to which Christ has entrusted the guardianship of the deposit of faith, is obstinately rejected. Each one is free to read and to understand Sacred Scripture according to one's personal interpretation. In this way, faith in the Word of God is destroyed. The work of the Antichrist, in this period of history, is the division of the Church and the consequent formation of new and numerous Christian Confessions which gradually become driven to a more and more extensive loss of the true faith in the word of God."

"666 indicated thrice, that is to say, for the third time, expresses the year 1998, nineteen hundred and ninety-eight. In this period of history, Freemasonry, assisted by its ecclesiastical form, will succeed in its great design: that of setting up an idol to put in the place of Christ and his Church. A false christ and a false church. Consequently, the statue built in honor of the first beast, to be adored by all the inhabitants of the earth and which will seal with its mark all those who want to buy or sell, is that of the Antichrist. You have thus arrived at the peak of the purification, of the great tribulation and of the apostasy. The apostasy will be, as of then, generalized because almost all will follow the false Christ and the false church. Then the door will be open for the appearance of the very person of the Antichrist" (Gobbi, 611-613, Message 407, Para. I-P).

6. FREEMASONRY, NEO-PAGANISM AND THE NEW WORLD ORDER

Freemasonry and the neo-paganism that it both espouses and promulgates pose, in our times, the most significant threat to Christianity in general and the Catholic Church in particular. In fact, the threat is so serious that the Blessed Mother has revealed, in her locutions to Fr. Gobbi of the *Marian Movement of Priests*, that we will, in our lifetime, witness the passion, crucifixion and apparent death of the Catholic Church, and ecclesiastical Freemasonry (that is, Freemasonry having infiltrated the very hierarchy of the Church) will succeed in setting up a false christ and a false church. Furthermore, according to reliable and Church-approved prophecies and private revelations, this will culminate in the "abomination of desolation" and will set the stage for the arrival or manifestation of the very person of the Antichrist.

It goes without saying that Satan and his cohort is and will be behind all of this. But the question remains, "What is Freemasonry" and "What do Freemasons in the highest levels or degrees of the religion (and it is a religion) believe?" The answers to these questions are difficult to obtain, as Masonry is an incredibly secretive society. One of the few things we do know about Masonry is that the secret society is broken into three levels: 1st Entered Apprentice; 2nd The Fellow Craft; 3rd Master Mason. The overwhelming majority of Freemasons belong to the first and second classes, and the "secrets" of Masonry are withheld from these members. Thus, many 1st and 2nd degree Masons are themselves ignorant of the secret origins and agenda of the 3rd level Master Masons. And among this elite class of Master Masons are some of the most brilliant, educated, powerful and wealthy members of society. These enormously powerful men truly are the puppet masters, pulling the strings and manipulating the political, economic, and ideological milieu. And contrary to the popular, widely held misconception that the United States of America was founded on Judeo-Christian principles, the United States, in truth, was founded on Masonic and deistic principles.

Masons founded this nation, and they believe that they can and should determine its future course, espousing and promoting ancient druid and pagan beliefs and rituals, astrology, the banishing of organized religion (specifically Christianity and the Roman Catholic Church), the implementation of a One World Government, genocide on a massive level, sterilization, control over reproduction and eugenics. Given the seriousness of the situation, it is imperative that Catholics be made aware of this devious agenda, and pray and work, under the leadership and protection of the Blessed Virgin Mary, to thwart the Masonic effort. Moreover, it is this author's contention that history cannot be properly understood without factoring in the significant role that these secret, elite and tremendously powerful societies have played behind the curtain and in the shadows. History needs to be re-written, taking into consideration the power and influence of said societies. Finally, the Blessed Mother, in her book, *To the Priests, Our Lady's Beloved Sons*, identifies Freemasonry as the black beast of the Book of Revelation, black precisely because in operates in the dark, in secrecy and behind the scenes. Later in this essay, there shall be provided a partial listing of prominent Freemasons, almost all of whom are common, household names.

Before we delve into the origins of Freemasonry, which essentially constitute the great "secrets" of the order, let us begin with a discussion of the concept of deism, for it is a well established fact that the overwhelming majority of the founding fathers were both Freemasons and deists, and that deism is one of the essential philosophies at the heart of the society's beliefs. Let us, then, explore this concept of deism. Wikipedia, the online dictionary, defines the term as follows:

"Deism in the philosophy of religion is the standpoint that reason and observation of the natural world, without the need for organized religion, can determine that the universe is a creation and has a creator. Furthermore, the term often implies that this Supreme Being does not intervene in human affairs or suspend the natural laws of the universe. Deists typically reject supernatural events such as prophecy and miracles, tending to assert that a god (or "the Supreme Architect") does not alter the universe by (regularly or ever) intervening in the affairs of human life. This idea is also known as the Clockwork universe theory, in which a god designs and builds the universe, but steps aside to let it run on its own. Deists believe in the existence of a god without any reliance on revealed religion, religious authority or holy books" (www.Wikipedia.com).

Based on this definition, we must understand very clearly from the outset that deism is at fundamental odds with Christianity. A deist denies that God ever has, could, or ever would intervene in human affairs. Thus, to the deist, such fundamental theological realities as the Incarnation, the divinity of Christ, all of the miracles attributed to Christ, etc., are utterly rejected and denied. Freemasons may say publicly that their society is not a religion, and that it's members can conceive of God however they would prefer to, but this is a lie. In fact, one of Freemasonry's primary objectives is to banish organized religion in general and Christianity in particular. The only logical conclusion that follows from their deistic beliefs is that they are anti-Christ, anti-Church, anti-Judeo-Christianity. Don't let the facade of their charitable causes fool you (such as the Shriner's Hospitals for children and burn victims). After all, they are carrying out their agenda under the guise of humanitarianism. Thus, what may appear from the outside to be something good, positive, and "humanitarian" is thoroughly corrupt at the core. There are very dark forces at play here, manipulating the minds of the masses. Moreover, we'd be absolute fools to think this most powerful group of men is not utilizing the tremendous information gathering technology that is at their disposal to assist in their sick selection and categorization processes that will ultimately determine your role in society, if you happen to be so luck as to have one. Let's not mince words. The Freemasons are in league with the Devil himself.

In essence, Masons espouse and promote a neo-paganism that seems to blend the disparate philosophies of deism, polytheism and pantheism. The deistic tendencies have been explained above. Additionally, this neo-paganism is polytheistic in its worship of many gods, such as geometry, reason, the sun and other celestial bodies, and ultimately, the human person. Finally, there is an element of pantheism, which is the belief that everything is a part of God. It is precisely this pantheistic belief that gives rise to the worship of nature, and, ultimately, to the worship of the human person, who is the highest expression of nature. Thus, the Freemasons, as neo-pagans, ultimately worship themselves, and this is the supreme deception of the anti-Christ: "The supreme religious deception is that of the Antichrist, a pseudo-messianism by which man glorifies himself in place of God and of his Messiah come in the flesh"(CCC, 675).

Speaking on implementing their agenda in the name of humanitarianism, author Fr. Robert Hugh Benson has this to say: "Humanitarianism...is becoming an actual religion itself, though anti-supernatural. It is a pantheism. Pantheism deifies all nature, God is the world, but naturally, man above all is God since he is the highest expression of nature. It is a religion devoid of the 'super' natural, because since God is nature itself, there is no longer a distinction between Creator and creature. The creature is God* and hence arbitrator of his own destiny and establishes the moral law for himself. Nature, and man is its highest expression, has all the divine attributes. Humanitarianism is a religion devoid of the supernatural. It is developing a ritual under Freemasonry; it has a creed, 'God is man'; and the rest. It has, therefore, a real food of a sort to offer religious cravings: it idealizes, and yet makes no demands upon the spiritual faculties. Then, they have the use of all the churches except ours, and of all the Cathedrals; and they are beginning at last to encourage sentiment. Then they may display their symbols and we may not: I think they will be established legally in another ten years" (Introduction, p. xvii).

Speaking on the new paganism, author and apologist Peter J. Kreeft, Ph.D., states in his book, *Fundamentals of the Faith,* that there are three significant differences between the pagans of ancient times and the neo-pagans of today. First, in ancient paganism, there existed an "instinct" to respect something greater than one's self. In other words, the ancients possessed humility, which is so egregiously lacking in neo-paganism. Second, the ancients subscribed to the philosophical conviction of moral absolutes. Modern paganism, quite to the contrary, is morally relativistic. The only absolute is that there are no absolutes, the only truth is that there is no such thing as truth, and the only thing that is wrong is the idea that anything at all is wrong. The third element of the old paganism that is missing from the new is a sense of worship, wonder and mystery. Even among the so-called "religious," we see a watering down of the sense of mystery and awe in present day liturgical worship services. In essence, the neo-pagan, unlike the pagans of old, presents with the symptoms of a radical narcissism in having rejected the divine revelation of God to humanity. In addition to the Masonic agenda to eradicate Judeo-Christian beliefs and practices, including, as stated above, the idea that there are any such things as moral absolutes, this relativistic agenda additionally includes the implementation of a New World Order founded on four recurring themes: (1) Dramatically reducing the population of the world; (2) Promoting environmentalism; (3) Establishing a world government; and (4) Promoting a new spirituality.

The Secrets of Freemasonry Decoded by Thomas Paine

Thomas Paine, American revolutionary and author, was himself a deist and espoused many of the tenets of Freemasonry, although it remains unknown to this author as to whether or not he was, himself, a Mason. He was, however, certainly in league with the Freemasons, and known for his espousal of occult beliefs and practices. In an essay he wrote entitled, "On the Freemasons," he assembles quotes from famous, high-ranking Freemasons that, when taken together, present a picture of what exactly Freemasonry is all about. Paine presents a number of salient quotations, which shall be here presented in Italics. The following essay is found in the *Life and Writings of Thomas Paine,* edited by Daniel Edwin Wheeler, 1908.

In his essay on Freemasonry, Paine states: "In 1730, Samuel Pritchard, member of a constituted lodge in England, published a treatise entitled 'Masonry Dissected'; and made oath before the Lord Mayor of London that it was a true copy....In his introduction he says, 'the original institution of Masonry consisted in the foundation of the liberal arts and sciences, but more especially in geometry, for at the building of the tower of Babel, the art and mystery of Masonry was first introduced, and from thence handed down by Euclid, a worthy and excellent mathematician of the Egyptians; and he communicated it to Hiram, the Master Mason concerned in building Solomon's Temple in Jerusalem....In 1783, Captain George Smith, inspector of the Royal Artillery Academy at Woolwich, in England, and Provincial Grand Master of Masonry for the County of Kent, published a treatise entitled, 'The Use and Abuse of Freemasonry.'

"In his chapter of the antiquity of Masonry, he makes it to be coeval with creation, 'when,' says he, 'the sovereign architect raised on Masonic principles the beauteous globe, and commanded the master science, geometry, to lay the planetary world, and to regulate by its laws the whole stupendous system in just, unerring proportion, rolling round the central sun.' 'But,' continues he, 'I am not at liberty publicly to undraw the curtain, and openly to descant on this head; it is sacred, and ever will remain so; those who are honored with the trust will not reveal it, and those who are ignorant of it cannot betray it....The learned, but unfortunate Doctor Dodd, Grand Chaplain of Masonry, in his oration at the dedication of Freemason's Hall, London, traces Masonry through a variety of stages. 'Masons,' says he, 'are well informed from their own private and interior records that the building of Solomon's Temple is an important era, from whence they derive many mysteries of their art.'"

"'Now,' says he, 'be it remembered that this great event took place above one thousand years before the Christian era, and consequently more than a century before Homer, the first of the Grecian poets, wrote; and about five centuries before Pythagoras brought from the East his sublime system of truly Masonic instruction to illuminate our western world. But, remote as this period is, we date not from thence the commencement of our art. For though it might owe to the wise and glorious King of Israel some of its many mystic forms and hieroglyphic ceremonies, yet certainly the art itself is coeval with man, the great subject of it.' 'We trace,' continues he, 'its footsteps in the most distant, the most remote ages and nations of the world. We find it among the first and most celebrated civilizers of the East. We deduce it regularly from the first astronomers on the plains of Chaldea, to the wise and mystic kings and priests of Egypt, the sages of Greece, and the philosophers of Rome.'"

At this point, Paine presents his thesis on the origins of Masonry, which are simultaneously bound up with the secrets, ceremonies, rituals, beliefs, and as we shall treat of later, the agenda of Freemasonry. It reads as follows: "From these reports and declarations of Masons of the highest order in the institution, we see that Masonry, without publicly declaring so, lays claim to some divine communications from the Creator, in a manner different from, and unconnected with, the book which the Christians call the Bible; and the natural result from this is, that Masonry is derived from some very ancient religion, wholly independent of and unconnected with that book. To come then at once to the point, Masonry (as I shall show from the customs, ceremonies, hieroglyphics, and chronology of Masonry) is derived and is the remains of the religion of the ancient Druids; who, like the magi of Persia and the priests of Heliopolis in Egypt, were priests of the sun. They paid worship to this great luminary, as the great visible agent of a great invisible first cause, whom they styled 'Time without limits.'"

The Blessed Mother, in, *To the Priests, Our Lady's Beloved Sons*, laments that the world has once again become pagan. This reality is largely the result of the profound influence that Freemasonry exercises in and throughout the world. Through the manipulation of the means of social communication, anti-Christian ideals are promoted and promulgated. In fact, humanity is currently undergoing a mass brainwashing, whereby the masses are led to believe that evil is good and good is evil. For instance, active homosexuality, which was rightly held to be gravely immoral for thousands of years, is now, suddenly, a natural, viable lifestyle and "gay marriage" should be embraced by all; those who oppose gay unions are labeled "homophobic" and are ostracized for their "antiquated" views on morality; all forms of sexual impurity and promiscuity are set up as the norm of human behavior; cheating, manipulation and the use of others for one's own advancement in society is seen as normal and even virtuous behavior; and the "dictatorship of moral relativism" is seen as a triumph in the Western world. And is it not ironic that moral relativists who preach "tolerance," which is simply a buzzword for relativism, are entirely intolerant of Christians and Christianity? Thus, we begin to understand why the Blessed Mother places the blame for the moral decline of civilization squarely on Freemasonry, the Great Beast of the Book of Revelation.

Rosicrucianism and the Georgia Guidestones

Again referring to Wikipedia, the online free, self-sustaining encyclopedia, the secret society of Rosicrucianism is defined as follows: Rosicrucianism is a philosophical secret society, said to have been founded in late medieval Germany by Christian Rosenkreuz. It holds a doctrine or theology "built on esoteric truths of the ancient past", which, "concealed from the average man, provide insight into nature, the physical universe and the spiritual realm." Rosicrucianism is symbolized by the Rosy Cross.

Does this sound familiar? Ties to the ancient pagan religions and ceremonies, "esoteric" truths known only to an elite few concerning the ultimate force of all things – Rosicrucianism is a secret society that has the same essential form of Freemasonry and is affiliated with Freemasonry. That connection having been made, we shall be in a better position to understand the significance of the phenomenon of the Georgia Guidestones. In June of 1979, a well-dressed and articulate man who went by the pseudonym of R.C. Christian walked into the Elberton Granite Finishing Company and commissioned the erection of a giant granite monument. He provided neither his own true identity, nor the identities of those involved in the commissioning of the project. The monument itself was to be consisted of four giant granite stones with 10 guides or "commandments" in eight different languages. Mr Christian stated that he wanted to have this monument built to transmit a message to all mankind and future generations. Five themes emerge as we read through these new 10 commandments: (1) The establishment of a new world order with a one world government; (2) Massive population reduction and control of reproduction, or eugenics; (3) Environmentalism and man's connection to nature; (4) A new world spirituality; (5) The worship or primacy of place given to Reason.

The Georgia Guidestones: The Ten Commandments of the New World Order

1. Maintain humanity under 500,000,000 in perpetual balance with nature.
2. Guide reproduction wisely – improving fitness and diversity.
3. Unite humanity with a living new language.
4. Rule passion – faith – tradition – and all things with tempered reason.
5. Protect people and nations with fair laws and just courts.
6. Let all nations rule internally resolving external disputes in a world court.

7. Avoid petty laws and useless officials.
8. Balance personal rights with social duties.
9. Prize truth – beauty – love – seeking harmony with the infinite.
10. Be not a cancer on the earth – Leave room for nature – Leave room for nature.

Moreover, the commandments are additionally inscribed in four ancient, dead languages: Babylonian Cuneiform, Classical Greek, Sanskrit and Egyptian Hieroglyphics.

All of this is no mere coincidence; it is all a part of a grand design that has been worked out in secret, behind closed doors by the most powerful men on earth. The inscription in the four dead languages harkens back to the ancient cultures that are revered by the Freemasons – the Ancient Egyptians, the Babylonians, the Ancient Greeks, and so on. These are the pagan cultures from which the Freemasons derive their beliefs, worship services and rituals.

What is more, in a book by the R.C. Christian, it is stated that the Guidestones were erected to pay homage to Thomas Paine and the occult philosophy he espoused. Thomas Paine wrote prolifically for the masses on such topics as a one world government, a new occult spirituality that would/should take the place of the prevailing and traditional, Judeo-Christian Spirituality, and many other themes that are entirely consonant with the beliefs and the agenda of the Freemasons.

Who are the Freemasons?

The question should be, "Who is not a Freemason?" A partial list is provided here courtesy of Wes Penre:

US-Presidents: George Washington, James Monroe, Andrew Jackson, James Polk, James Buchanan, Andrew Johnson, James Garfield, William McKinley, Theodore Roosevelt, William Howard Taft, Warren G. Harding, Franklin D. Roosevelt, Harry S. Truman, Lyndon B. Johnson, Gerald R. Ford.

Political leaders worldwide: Winston Churchill, Simon Bolivar, Edmund Burke, Benito Juarez, Edward VII, George VI, Bernardo O'Higgins, José de San Martin, Francisco de Paula Santander, José Rizal, José Marti, Pandit Nehru, Lajos Kossuth, Jonas Furrer, Guiseppe Mazzini, Eduard Benes, John A. MacDonald, Aaron Burr, George McGovern, Barry Goldwater, Estes Kefauer, Thomas E. Dewey,

Alf Landon, Hubert H. Humphrey, Wendel Wilke, W.E.B. DuBois, William Jennings Bryant, King Hussein of Jordan, Yasser Arafat, Francois Mitterand, Helmut Kohl, Gerhard Shroeder, Tony Blair, Yikzak Rabbin, Cecil Rhodes, Sir John J.C. Abbott, Stephen F. Austin, John G. Diefenbaker, Samuel J. Ervin Jr. (Watergate committee), Benjamin Franklin, John Hancock, Patrick Henry, Rev. Jesse Jackson, Sam Nunn, Lowell Thomas (brough Lawrence of Arabia to pub. not.), Gov. George C. Wallace, Strom Thurman, Jesse Helms, Robert Dole, Jack Kemp, Al Gore, Prince Phillip (GB), Zbigniew Brzezinski, Lord Peter Carrington, Andrew Carnegie, W. Averell Harriman, Henry Kissinger, Richard D. Heideman, Robert McNamara.

Military leaders: Omar Bradley, John J. Pershing, Douglas McArthur, General Winfield Scott, Captain Eddie Rickenbacker, Jimmy Doolittle, General Mark Clarkem General George C. Marshall, General Henry "Hap" Arnold, John Paul Jones, Afred von Tirpitz (submarine warfare).

Artists and entertainers: W.A. Mozart, Leopold Mozart, Ludwig van Beethoven, Jean Sibelius, Franz Liszt, Josef Haydn, Irving Berlin, Gutzon Borglum, Charles Peale, Alfons M. Mucha, Richard Wagner, John Philip Sousa, Gilbert & Sullivan, George Gershwin, George M. Cohen, Count Basie, Louise Armstrong, Nat King Cole, Giacomo Meyerbeer, Sigmund Romberg, John Wayne, Red Skelton, Clarke Gable, W.C. Fields, Will Rogers, Burl Ives, Roy Rogers, Danny Thomas, Ernest Borgnine, Oliver Hardy, Tom Mix, Audie Murphy, Gene Autry, Wallace Beery, Eddie Cantor, Roy Clarke, George M. Cohan, Walt Disney, Duke Ellington, Douglas Fairbanks, Leonardo da Vinci, Arthur Godfrey, Bob Hope, Harry Houdini, Al Jolson, Elmo Lincoln (Tarzan), Harold C. Lloyd,.jr, Tom Mix, Ronald Reagan, Will Rogers, Peter Sellers, William Shakespeare, Charles "Tom Thumb" Stratton, Paul Whiteman (King of Jazz), William Wyler (dir. of Ben Hur), Cecil B. DeMille, Sir Arthur Sullivan, John Zoffany.

Movie industry: Jack Warner, Louise B. Mayer (MGM), Darryl F. Zanuck (20th Century Fox).

Industry, trady, banking and labor: Henry Ford, Samuel Gompers, Walter P. Chrysler, John Wanamaker, S.S. Kresge, J.C. Penney, John Jacob Astor, John L. Lewis, Pehr G. Gyllenhammar (Volvo), Percy Barnevik (ABB), André Citroën, Samuel Colt (Colt revolver), Edwin L. Drake (oil), Rockefeller family, Rothschild family, King C. Gillette (Razors), Charles C. Hilton (Hilton hotels), Sir Thomas Lipton (Tea), Harry S. New (Airmail), Ransom E. Olds (Oldsmobile), David Sarnoff (father of TV), John W. Teets, Dave Thomas (Wendy's Rest.), Edgar Bronfman Jr. (Seagram Whiskey), Rich DeVos (Amway), Alan Greenspan (Fed. Reserve), Giovanni Agnelli (FIAT), Peter Wallenberg (SE-Bank Sweden).

Adventurers: Lewis & Clarke, Charles A. Lindbergh, Kit Carson, Roald Amundsen, Admiral Richard Byrd, Commodore Robert Peary, Kit Carson, Casanova, William "Buffalo Bill" Cody, Davy Crockett, Meriwether Lewis, Robert E. Peary (Northpole).

Philosophers: Johann Wolfgang von Goethe, Gotthold E. Lessing, Voltaire.

Astronauts: Buzz Aldrin, Leroy Gordon Cooper, Donn Eisele, Virgil I. Grissom, Edgar D. Mitchell, Walter Schirra Jr., Thomas P. Stafford, Paul Weitz, James Irvin, John Glenn.

Writers: Mark Twain, Sir Walter Scott, Rudyard Kipling, Robert Burns, Wassily I. Maikow, Heinrich Heine, Jean P.C. de Florian, Leopoldo Lugoner, Antonio de Castro Alves, James Boswell, Alexander Pushkin, Sir Arthur Conan Doyle, Jonathan Swift, Oscar Wilde, Jules Verne, H.G. Wells, Robert Burns, Carlo Collodi (Pinoccio), Edward Gibbon, Francis Scott Key (US NAtional Anthem), Rudyard Kipling, Felix Salten (Bambi), Lewis Wallace (Ben Hur), Alexander Pope.

Medicine: Alexander Fleming (Penicillin), Jules Bordet, Antoine DePage, Edward Jenner, Charles & William Mayo, Karl & William Menninger, Karl A. Menninger (psychiatrist), Andrew T. Still (Osteopathy).

Science: Carl Sagan, Hans C. Orsted, J.J Frk. von Berzelius, Alfred Edmund Brehms, Luther Burbank, Johan Ernst Gunnerus, Albert Abraham Michelson (measured speed of light), Gaspard Monge, C.F.S. Hahnemann, Pedro N. Arata, Alexandre Gustave Eiffel, Jame Smithson, John Fitch (Steamboats), Joseph Ignance Guillotin (inventor of the Guillotin), Edward Jenner (vaccin), Simon Lake (submarine), Franz Anton Mesmer (Hypnotism), Albert Einstein, A.J. Sax (saxophone).

Law: Henry Baldwin, Hugo L. Black, John Blair Jr., Samuel Blatchford, Harold H. Burton, James F. Byrnes, John Catton, Thomas C. Clarke, John H. Clarke, William Cushing, Willis van Devanter, William O. Douglas, Oliver Ellsworth, Stephen J. Field, John M. Harlan, RObert H. Jackson, Joseph E. Lamar, Thurgood Marshall, Stanley Matthews, Sherman Minton, Tom Mix, William H. Moody, Samuel Nelson, William Paterson,

Mahlon Pitney, Stanley F. Reed, Wiley B. Rutledge, Potter Stewart, Noah H. Swayne, Thomas Todd, Robert Trimble, Frederick M. Vinson, Earl Warren, Levi Woodbury, William B. Woods.

Others: Frederic A. Bartholdi (designed the Staue of Liberty), Daniel Carter Beard (founder of Boy Scouts), Cornelius Hedges (Yellowstone Nat.Park), James Hoban (architect U.S Captial), James Naismith (basketball), Paul Revere (famous American), Rupert Murdoch (media mogul).

Education: Robert E.B. Baylor, Leland Stanford (Railroads & Stanford University).

Religious leaders: Father Francisco Calvo (Jesuit Cat.. Priest), Geoffrey Fisher (Canterbury), Billy Graham, Rev. Jesse Jackson, Joseph Fort Newton, Robert Shuller, Oral Roberts, Louise Farrahkan (Nation of Islam), G. Bromley Oxman (friend of Billy Graham), Joseph Smith (Mormon cult), Hyrum Smith (Brother), Brigham Young (2nd leader of Mormon cult), Sidney Rigdon (early Mormon), Heber C. Kimball, Spencer Kimball, Aleister Crowley (Satanist), Gerald B. Gardner (Wiccan), Wynn Westcott (Golden Dawn).

Organizations: Jean Henry Dunant (Red Cross), Melvin Jones (Lions Int.), Giuseppe Mazzini (Ital. Illuminati leader), Albert Pike (Ku Klux Klan).

Intelligence: J. Edgar Hoover, William Casey.

The Church and Freemasonry: Still Vehemently Prohibited

"The denomination with the longest history of objection to Freemasonry is the Roman Catholic Church. The objections raised by the Roman Catholic Church are based on the allegation that Masonry teaches a naturalistic deistic religion which is in conflict with Church doctrine. A number of Papal pronouncements have been issued against Freemasonry. The first was Pope Clement XII's *In Eminenti*, 28 April 1738; the most recent was Pope Leo XIII's *Ab Apostolici*, 15 October 1890. The 1917 Code of Canon Law explicitly declared that joining Freemasonry entailed automatic excommunication. The 1917 Code of Canon Law also forbade books friendly to Freemasonry" (www.wikipedia.com).

"In 1983, the Church issued a new Code of Canon Law. Unlike its predecessor, it did not explicitly name Masonic orders among the secret societies it condemns. It states in part: "A person who joins an association which plots against the Church is to be punished with a just penalty; one who promotes or takes office in such an association is to be punished with an interdict." This named omission of Masonic orders caused both Catholics and Freemasons to believe that the ban on Catholics becoming Freemasons may have been lifted, especially after the perceived liberalisation of Vatican II. However, the matter was clarified when Cardinal Joseph Ratzinger (later Pope Benedict XVI), as the Prefect of the Congregation for the Doctrine of the Faith, issued *Quaesitum est*, which states: "... the Church's negative judgment in regard to Masonic association remains unchanged since their principles have always been considered irreconcilable with the doctrine of the Church and therefore membership in them remains forbidden. The faithful who enroll in Masonic associations are in a state of grave sin and may not receive Holy Communion." Thus, from a Catholic perspective, there is still a ban on Catholics joining Masonic Lodges" (*ibid.*).

7. THE TRIUMPH OF THE IMMACULATE HEART OF MARY AND THE GLORIOUS REIGN OF CHRIST ON EARTH

It is clear from what we have read that we are, in fact, living throughout the final-phase of the end-times, prophesied in St. John's Book of the Apocalypse, where the "woman clothed with the sun," Mary, and the "huge Red Dragon," Lucifer, are engaged in a cosmic warfare for human souls. The huge Red Dragon has spewed a torrent of water at the Woman, the torrent representing all the attempts to theoretically and practically debase the Woman and devotion to her. In response, the Woman has taken to flight on the two wings of the eagle, which represent faith and charity, and has taken up refuge in the desert of the souls of her consecrated children, both priests and laity. In the desert of those souls entrusted totally to her, she is performing her greatest prodigies and miracles of grace, silently and in a hidden fashion bringing these souls to great sanctity without the consecrated persons even being aware of what is happening. She is forming them by adorning them with her own virtues and cultivating within them fervent prayer and heroic suffering for the glory of God and the salvation of souls. These humble souls make up, here on earth, the humble "heel" with which she shall crush the head of the ancient serpent who is the devil and Satan. In heaven, they shall make up her crown of luminous stars.

We are living through the "Tribulation" and the "Purification," a time in history when the Antichrist, whose number and name is 666, is successfully seducing the world through a great apostasy – a wide-spread, widely diffused rejection of the true faith in favor of theoretical and practical atheism. Chapter 12 of the Apocalypse refers to Satan in these, the "latter-days," as "the Huge Red Dragon," and this due to the fact that, as prophesied at Fatima, Russia has indeed spread its error of Marxist atheism. Also at Fatima, Mary came with the antidote for these times: total consecration of the world to the Immaculate Heart of Mary by the Pope and all the bishops united with him. Unfortunately, despite sincere attempts by Blessed Pope John Paul II, this did not happen as a consequence of bishops not taking this request of Our Lady and the Holy Father seriously. It will happen, as the Blessed Mother herself has prophesied, but only after humanity is already within the bloody persecution of the Church. Consecration to Her Heart is still the answer, as we have already seen.

Moreover, the Church, the Mystical Body of Christ, like its head, is undergoing its own passion and crucifixion, being attacked from without and from within. The attack on the Church from without is Marxist Atheism, the "huge Red Dragon." The task of the huge Red Dragon is to promote the ideology of Marxist atheism, while the task of the Black Beast, or Freemasonry, is that of blaspheming God. It does this by promoting the violation of each of the Ten Commandments as something good or "politically correct." Thus, as Mary has stated in many of her messages, "Evil has become good, and good has become evil." This constitutes the greatest Blasphemy of God's law of love.

Additionally, the Beast like a Lamb with two horns is ecclesiastical Masonry, whose function is that of establishing a false Christ and a false church. The symbol of the two horns is intimately connected with the priesthood of both the Old and New Testaments. Ecclesiastical Masonry is insidious in that it denies the historical Christ by favoring naturalistic and purely rational forms of exegesis (explanations of the Gospel), eventually calling into question the veracity of the miracles performed by Christ. Ultimately, the miracle of the resurrection itself is called into question by these ultra-liberal exegetes and theologians, thereby stripping Jesus of His divinity.

Yet Mary has foretold and promised Her Triumph; what is more, she has unequivocally stated in numerous messages to Fr. Gobbi that the Triumph of Her Immaculate Heart will coincide with the Glorious reign of Christ. But what exactly are we to make of this? Is the Blessed Mother speaking of the Final Judgment to take place at the end of time? Interestingly, the Church has very little to say officially about the return of Christ. I will make the argument that Fr Gobbi makes in his booklet, *The Triumph, The Second Coming and the Eucharistic Reign*, namely, that there will, in fact, be a Return of Christ in Glory to establish upon the earth His glorious reign of love, justice and peace. This will constitute the "new springtime" spoken of so frequently and prophetically by Blessed Pope John Paul II the Great. It was also John Paul II who spoke of us living through a "New Advent." Advent, theologically, is that period of time prior to the coming of Christ. We celebrate Advent each liturgical year in preparation for the coming of the Christ–Child, as if to re-live the first and greatly anticipated Advent. But John Paul II made it clear that the end of the 20th Century and the beginning of the 21st Century constituted the time of the "New Advent." What could this mean except that we're living on the threshold of a great hope – the hope of Christ's glorious return to earth!

Let us begin with an examination of the messages. From the very beginning of Mary's messages to Fr. Gobbi – December 24, 1975 - she explicitly states the following: "Do not fear: as my Heart has given you the Savior, so now in these times my Immaculate Heart gives you the joy of salvation. Soon the whole world, which is pervaded with darkness and which has been snatched from my Son, will at last rejoice over the fruit of this Holy Night. The Triumph of my Immaculate Heart will be realized through a new birth of Jesus in the hearts and the souls of my poor wandering children. Only have confidence, and do not let anxiety or discouragement take hold of you. The future that awaits you will be a new dawn of light for the whole world, now at last made clean."

In fact, it seems that on the Holy night, the eve of Christmas day, Mary, in her messages to Fr. Gobbi, speaks of the Second Coming of Christ. On December 24, 1978, she gives an explicit message regarding this theme: "His second coming, beloved children, will be like the first. As was His birth on this night, so also will be the return of Jesus in glory…The world will be completely covered in the darkness of the denial of God, of its obstinate rejection of Him and of rebellion against His Law of Love. The coldness of hatred will still cause the roadways of this world to be deserted. Almost no one will be ready to receive Him. The great ones will not even remember Him, the rich will close their doors on Him, while his own will be too busy with seeking and affirming themselves…'When the Son of Man comes, will He still find faith on the earth?' (Lk 18:8). He will come suddenly, and the world will not be ready for his coming. He will come for a judgement for which man will find himself unprepared. He will come to establish his kingdom in the world, after having defeated and annihilated his enemies. Even in this second coming, the Son will come to you through his Mother. As the Word of the Father made use of my virginal womb to come to you, so also will Jesus make use of my Immaculate Heart to come and reign in your midst…" (166).

Speaking on this point, Fr. Gobbi states, "Since the triumph is the culmination of a great victory, only when Christ obtains his great victory will the Immaculate Heart of Mary triumph. And Christ will obtain his final and great victory with his return in glory. So now I understand why, in her messages, Our Lady says: 'The triumph of my Immaculate Heart will coincide with the return of Christ in glory.'" Based on the messages, we can begin to understand that Mary's triumph is Christ's triumph in glory on earth. But this can pose some confusion while, as stated earlier, the Church has traditionally identified the second coming with the "Parousia," or the final judgment. For clarification on this issue, let us turn to sacred Scripture and Sacred Tradition.

Scripturally, we find references throughout the Gospels that seem to speak to a second coming of Christ that refers specifically to the Parousia – or the judgment. For instance, in Mt 25:35-41, Jesus states, "You gave the hungry to eat, the thirsty to drink, you clothed the naked, you visited [the sick]. You who have done this to me – to my right. And you who have not done this – to my left." This is a clear reference to the final judgment. The only options for those on the right and on the left are heaven or hell. Yet there are other Scripture passages that seem necessarily to indicate a return of Christ to the earth before the Parousia.

There is the instance in Scripture when Christ was asked by Caiaphas, "Are you the Son of God?" Jesus' reply is, "Yes, I am, and you will see the Son of Man coming on the clouds of heaven in the splendor of his glory." (Mt 26:64). Moreover, we have already alluded to Christ's question, "When the Son of Man returns, will he still find faith on the earth?" Obviously, he cannot return to earth if there is no earth to return to at the end of time, when the only possibilities will be heaven or hell! Finally, we have the account of the ascension, when the angels say, "Galileans, what are you doing? Just as you have seen him ascend, so too will you see him return in the splendor of his glory, on the clouds of heaven." (Acts 1:11).

At this point, Fr. Gobbi addresses another significant point in Scripture, namely a passage from the Book of the Apocalypse "which talks about a great persecution." (Rev 20:1-7). Many will perish due to this persecution, which ties in with the prophecies of Fatima, Akita, and La Salette, but Christ will defeat his enemy, and the Adversary will be bound and cast into hell, where he will no longer be capable of harming the human race. Rev 20:3 states, "The door of the abyss will be closed so that he may no longer harm the world." Fr. Gobbi continues on to state that some of the individuals who die during the great persecution "will rise again to reign with Christ." This ties in with the prophecy of La Salette. Some of these individuals who will die as martyrs will experience a first resurrection. A second, humanity-wide, resurrection will take place at the end of time, when Christ separates the sheep from the goats. Thus, the end of Satan's power, then, is the triumph of the Immaculate Heart, which coincides with the triumph of Jesus Christ to establish his glorious reign on the face of the earth!

There is additionally abundant Magisterial support for this belief concerning a second glorious coming of Christ on earth. Fr. Gobbi quotes Blessed John Paul II, stating, as recorded by "Osservatore Romano," September 27, 1984, "May the God of peace be with us, here in Canada and everywhere. May justice and peace kiss once again at the end of the Second Millennium, which is preparing us for Christ's coming in glory." Moreover, on August 15, 1993, at the conclusion of his World Youth Day homily in Denver, the Pope stated the following: "This pilgrimage must continue – it must continue in our lives; it must continue in the life of the Church as She looks to the Third Christian Millennium. It must continue as a new advent, a moment of hope and expectation, until the return of the Lord in glory. Your celebration of this World Youth Day has been a pause along the journey, a moment of prayer and of refreshment, but our journey must take us even further, even to the return of the Lord in glory!"

To conclude with an official pronouncement, Fr. Gobbi was made aware of the fact that a very specific eschatological question was put to the Congregation for the Doctrine of the Faith, then headed by Joseph Cardinal Ratzinger, now Pope Benedict XVI. The question was, "Is the return of Christ in glory to be interpreted as his return for the Last Judgment, or rather on this earth?" The answer provided by the CDF was, "The Church has never taken an official stand on this subject, therefore one can interpret either way." Fr. Gobbi concludes this section with the following words: "I have shown you the reasons for which, according to Scripture and according to the teaching of the Church, we tend to support the second interpretation – that the return of Christ in glory will take place on this earth." Furthermore, according to Fr. Gobbi, the hallmarks or characteristics of this second glorious return of Christ will be four-fold: (1) The first petition of the "Our Father Prayer" will be realized…"Thy kingdom come, Thy Will be done, on earth, as it is in heaven;" (2) It will coincide with the Second Pentecost, spoken of earlier; (3) It will be the greatest manifestation or act of God's merciful love; (4) The Triumph of the Immaculate Heart and the second glorious coming of Christ will usher in the "Eucharistic Reign" of Christ (Gobbi, 1996).

8. MEDIATRIX AND CONSECRATION IN PRIVATE REVELATION

Mary as Mediatrix to Fr. Gobbi

In message 204 of *To the Priests, Our Lady's Beloved Sons,* the Blessed Mother reveals the following about her role as Mediatrix, which, as we shall see in Section II, is the firm theological foundation for Marian Consecration. Here, she explains that she is only capable of fully carrying out her role as Mediatrix of Grace with respect to those souls who have fully consecrated or entrusted themselves to her. Thus, the consecration is our "Fiat," our "Yes" to Mary, enabling her to perform her greatest miracles of grace within the desert of our souls. She states, "Beloved Children, I am the Mediatrix of Graces. Grace is the very life of God which is communicated to you. It springs from the bosom of the Father and is merited for you by the Word who, in my virginal womb, became man to share with you that same divine life, and for this He offered Himself as a ransom for you, becoming thus the one and only Mediator between God and all humanity" (Gobbi, 269-70, Message 204, Para. A-O).

"From the bosom of the father, grace, in order to reach you, must therefore pass through the divine Heart of the Son, who communicates it to you in His Spirit of Love. Just as a ray of light, which passes through a window, assumes its shape, color and design, so too divine grace, merited by Jesus, can come to you only through Him, and it is for this reason that it reproduces in you his own image, the very same image which shapes you ever more and more to his own person. Divine life can reach you only in the form of Jesus, and the more this increases in you, the more you are assimilated to Him, in such a way that you can really grow as his little brothers. By means of Grace, the Father communicates Himself to you ever more and more, the Son assimilates you, the Holy Spirit transforms you, bringing about a relationship of life with the Most Holy Trinity, which becomes ever increasingly strong and active. Within souls who are in grace, it is the Most Holy Trinity Itself which takes up its dwelling place there. This life of grace has also a relationship with your heavenly Mother" (*ibid.*).

"As I am truly the Mother of Jesus and your Mother, my mediation is exercised between you and my Son Jesus. This is the natural consequence of my divine motherhood. As the Mother of Jesus, I am the means chosen by God by which my Son can reach you. In my virginal womb, this first act of mediation of mine is carried out. As your Mother, I was the means chosen by Jesus that through me all of you may reach Him. I am truly the Mediatrix of Grace between you and my Son Jesus. My task is that of distributing to my little children that grace which flows out from the bosom of the Father, is merited for you by the Son and is given to you by the Holy Spirit. My task is that of distributing it to all my children, according to the particular needs of each one, which the Mother is very good at knowing" (*ibid.*).

"I am ever carrying out this duty of mine. However I can carry it out fully only in the case of those children who entrust themselves to me with perfect abandonment. I am above all able to carry it out in respect to you, my favorite [children] who, by your consecration, have entrusted yourselves completely to me. I am the way which leads you to Jesus. I am the safest and shortest way, the necessary way for each one of you. If you refuse to go along this way, you run the danger of being lost in the course of your journey….Entrust yourselves to me with great confidence, and you will remain faithful, because I will be able to carry out fully my work as Mediatrix of all Graces. I will take you each day along the way of my Son, in such a way that He may increase in you to His fullness…." (*ibid.*). Finally, Mary as Mediatrix of all graces constitutes the firm theological foundation upon which Marian consecration rests. We will probe this in depth, in the forthcoming sections of this book.

"I Ask for the Consecration of All"

As has been stated numerous times thus far, Mary is, above all, asking her spiritual children to make a solemn act of consecration to her Immaculate Heart. When one consecrates himself to the Blessed Virgin, he is protecting himself from philosophical and theological error, he is assured of his salvation – a most consoling reality given the Satanic nature of the world in which we live, he is offering himself as an oblation, a victim, immolated on the altar of Mary's Immaculate Heart, through, with and in Jesus Christ, and this for the Glory of God and the salvation of souls. Marian consecration is the antidote for our times, for, as is stated in Rev. 12:14, "And there were given to the woman two wings of a great eagle, that she might fly into the desert unto her place."

As we have seen, the desert represents the desert of our souls, where Mary takes up residence through consecration to her, and there performs her greatest prodigies. Speaking on this, Mary states to Fr. Gobbi that, "In the desert, your hearts will be made ever purer by me that, in the light of wisdom, you may see the plan of the Father and, as did Jesus, you too may dispose yourselves to carry it out, drinking to the last drop the chalice which has already been prepared for you....For this, your hearts will have to be still more purified by me. The desert is the place where I bring you for this, my motherly work of purification" (Gobbi, Message 195). Thus, these clients of Mary reach great sanctity in a short period of time.

St. Louis de Montfort worked zealously to promote what he considered to be the ultimate path to sanctity and holiness – true devotion to Mary. And the highest expression of this true devotion to Mary was and is total consecration to her. The forthcoming section of this book is devoted to explaining in detail de Montfort's consecration to Mary. There are a few very important things to keep in mind as we read through the remainder of the text in order to have a complete picture of God's providential plan for the twentieth century with Mary as the leader of God's army in the cosmic battle between the "Woman clothed with the Sun" and the "great Red Dragon," or Lucifer and his minions.

De Montfort possessed the true wisdom of God, and, as a consequence, he was given to understand the tremendously sanctifying devotion of total consecration. He was the first saint to offer a comprehensive explanation of the nature of and motives for consecrating one's self to Mary. Moreover, he was imbued with the spirit of prophecy, prophetically writing that in the latter-days, God would rise up an army of great saints, all totally consecrated to Mary and imbued with her spirit. Speaking on this, de Montfort, who lived in the 18th Century, made the following prophetic statements regarding these apostles of the end-times:

"...Towards the end of the world, ...Almighty God and His holy Mother are to raise up saints who will surpass in holiness most other saints as much as the cedars of Lebanon tower above little shrubs. These great souls filled with grace and zeal will be chosen to oppose the enemies of God who are raging on all sides. They will be exceptionally devoted to the Blessed Virgin. Illumined by her light, strengthened by her spirit, supported by her arms, sheltered under her protection, they will fight with one hand and build with the other. With one hand they will give battle, overthrowing and crushing heretics and their heresies, schismatics and their schisms, idolaters and their idolatries, sinners and their wickedness. With the other hand they will build the temple of the true Solomon and the mystical city of God, namely, the Blessed Virgin. They will be like thunderclouds flying through the air at the slightest breath of the Holy Spirit. Attached to nothing, surprised at nothing, they will shower down the rain of God's word and of eternal life. They will thunder against sin; they will storm against the world; they will strike down the devil and his followers and for life and for death, they will pierce through and through with the two-edged sword of God's word all those against whom they are sent by Almighty God. They will be true apostles of the latter times to whom the Lord of Hosts will give eloquence and strength to work wonders and carry off glorious spoils from His enemies. They will sleep without gold or silver and, more important still, without concern in the midst of other priests, ecclesiastics and clerics. Yet they will have the silver wings of the dove enabling them to go wherever the Holy Spirit calls them, filled as they are, with the resolve to seek the glory of God and the salvation of souls. Wherever they preach, they will leave behind them nothing but the gold of love, which is the fulfillment of the whole law. They will have the two-edged sword of the Word of God in their mouths and the bloodstained standard of the Cross on their shoulders. They will carry the Crucifix in their right hand and the rosary in their left, and the holy names of Jesus and Mary on their heart."

It is important to note, in keeping with the radical interconnectedness of Mary's plan, that Blessed John Paul II was profoundly influenced by the writings of de Montfort, so much so that his papal motto and coat-of-arms both have their origin in de Montfort's writings and prayer of consecration. Moreover, St. Louis de Montfort refers to Marian consecration as the safest, surest, easiest, most secure and quickest route to sanctity and perfect conformity to the crucified love – Jesus Christ. We are called to imitate Christ in all things; let us, then, in imitation of Our Lord, become little children and entrust ourselves, with all of our many needs, to our and His Mother Mary. That good Mother encourages us explicitly to consecrate ourselves to her, whatever our particular state in life might be, and through the consecration, she will be enabled to exercise fully her role as Mediatrix with respect to our souls. Thus, she will form us into faithful replicas of her crucified Son. The following message given via interior locution to Fr. Gobbi, message #287, has Mary inviting us all to consecration:

"Consider the ineffable moment of the Annunciation made by the Archangel Gabriel, sent by God to receive my *yes* for the realization of his eternal plan of redemption, and for the great mystery of the incarnation of the Word in my virginal womb, and then you will understand why I ask you to consecrate yourselves to my Immaculate Heart. Yes, I myself manifested my wish at Fatima, when I appeared in 1917; I have asked it many times of my daughter, Sister Lucy, who is still on earth for the accomplishment of this mission I have entrusted to her; during these years I have insistently requested it through the message entrusted to my sacerdotal Movement; today I renew my request that all be consecrated to my Immaculate Heart. Before all I ask it of Pope John Paul II, the first of my beloved sons, who on the occasion of this feast, performed the consecration in a solemn manner, after writing to the bishops of the world and inviting them to do so in union with him" (Gobbi, Message 287).

"Unfortunately, the invitation was not welcomed by all the bishops; particular circumstances have not yet permitted the explicit consecration of Russia which I have requested many times. As I have already told you, this consecration will be made to me when the bloody events are well on the way to actuality. I bless this courageous act of my Pope in his wish to entrust the world and all the nations to my Immaculate Heart; I receive it with love and gratitude, and because of it I promise to intervene to shorten greatly the hours of the purification and to lessen the gravity of the trial. But I ask this consecration also from all the bishops, from all the priests, from all religious, and from all the faithful. This is the hour in which the whole Church must assemble in the secure refuge of my Immaculate Heart" (*ibid.*).

We see how, as explained in the above message, Mary shortened the duration and lessened the intensity of the purification as a consequence of Blessed John Paul II's effort to consecrate the world to Mary's Immaculate Heart. If this was the case, imagine what Our Lady has in store for the Church and the world when the Church dogmatically recognizes her three-fold function as Co-Redemptrix, Mediatrix and Advocate.

9. THEOLOGY OF TOTAL CONSECRATION TO MARY

Having explored various Church-approved Marian private revelations as they pertain to the times through which we are currently living, we have found that the key to the Blessed Mother's plan to save humanity in general, and each soul in particular, is nothing other than total consecration to Her Immaculate Heart. For, Marian consecration is the apex of authentic, theologically sound devotion to the Mother of God. Moreover, it is the antidote to the widespread disease of apostasy, which, as we know from Mary's messages, is the great Red Dragon of Marxist Atheism. Additionally, the tremendous grace of salvation is promised to those who make and live such a consecration. Attempting to make it through these times in which we live without the protection, intercession, advocacy and mediation of Mary is perilous at the least, and such a soul seriously risks falling prey to the many and varied enticements of Satan that lurk around every corner. It is the purpose of this second section to study the essence of this devotion of Marian consecration, our much-needed protection in these latter-times. We will begin with an exploration of Mary as Mediatrix of all grace, the firm theological foundation for Marian consecration. Next, we will study St. Louis de Montfort's explanation of the nature and motives of the devotion. Finally, we will turn our attention to St. Joseph's role in this devotion, focusing first on his spousal union with Mary as the ultimate model of total consecration, secondly on his role as "spiritual father" and protector of the mystical body, and finally on the universality of Joseph as a model of holiness.

Mary Mediatrix of All Grace

To understand the logic of total consecration to Jesus through Mary, we must first grasp Mary's role as Mediatrix of all graces. This is the Church's doctrine that every grace that comes to us from God comes through the willed intercession of Mary. But this role of Mary as Mediatrix of all grace is really the completion of her role as Spiritual Mother, and follows from her unique cooperation in the redemption of humanity with Christ on Calvary. So let us first review these two concepts of Mary as Spiritual Mother and Co-Redemptrix.

A. SPIRITUAL MOTHER
1. Scripture
We find in Sacred Scripture two primary sources for our understanding of Mary as Spiritual Mother. The first is the passage of the Annunciation (Lk. 1:26). In giving her assent to become mother of Christ the Head, she also necessarily becomes mother of the body, the Church, which cannot be separated from that head. The second is Jn. 19:26 and following, which reads: "When Jesus saw his mother and the disciple whom he loved standing near, he said to his mother, "Woman, behold your son.""Then he said to the disciple, 'Behold your mother'" (Jn. 19:26-27). Dr. Mark Miravalle, contemporary Mariologist, explains that here the dying Jesus is not offering a suggestion but rather is stating a theological fact about Mary's relationship to John, whom Church Tradition has consistently taught represents all of humanity (Miravalle, 60-61).

2. Tradition
There is also clear evidence within Church Tradition of constant recourse to Mary as Spiritual Mother, beginning with the Church Fathers - who saw Mary as the New Eve, mother of all the spiritually living, - right up to the present pontificate of Pope Benedict XVI. We read in the Second Vatican Council document, *Lumen Gentium*, "Thus, in a wholly singular way she cooperated by her obedience, faith, hope, and burning charity in the work of the Savior in restoring supernatural life to souls. For this reason she is a mother to us in the order of grace" (*Lumen Gentium*, No. 61). Furthermore, Miravalle points out that "since Pope Sixtus IV (in 1477), no less than twenty-seven subsequent popes have declared Mary as Spiritual Mother with an always increasing specificity and clarity" (Miravalle, 62).

3. Theology of Spiritual Motherhood
The theology of Mary's Spiritual Motherhood is rooted in St. Paul's doctrine on the Church as Mystical Body of Christ. As was previously stated, Mary, in giving birth to Christ the Head, also gave birth to the body connected to that Head, which is the Church. Thus, Mary, in giving birth to the source of all grace, can rightly be called "Spiritual Mother" of all who benefit from that grace.

B. CO-REDEMPTRIX
1. From the Incarnation to the foot of the Cross
We have explained how Mary gave birth to the Church at the time of the Annunciation. But our analysis of Mary's Spiritual Motherhood would be incomplete without an understanding of her presence at the foot of the cross. It is true that Mary, in giving birth to the source of all grace,

participated in giving spiritual life to all those alive with that grace, and therefore can be called our Spiritual Mother. But Mary most fully became our mother at the foot of the cross where she, in a completely singular way, participated in the redemption of humanity with Christ. It is for this reason that the Church ascribes to her the title "Co-redemptrix."

2. *Lumen Gentium*

The "co" here in no way is meant to imply "equal with," for Vatican II makes very clear that Mary's cooperation in the redemption is entirely dependent upon and subordinate to Christ's perfect redemptive act. Nonetheless, God willed that just as the first Eve participated in bringing about the fall, so too should Mary, the new Eve, participate in the restoration of humanity with Christ, the new Adam. Mary's participation in the redemption is accomplished in two ways then: first, through the Incarnation, and secondly, at the foot of the cross. In the Incarnation, Mary provides Jesus with His body - the instrument of the redemption, just as Eve provided Adam with the fruit as the instrument of the fall. At the foot of the cross, united with the sacrifice of Christ, "Mary offered the maternal rights of her Son on the cross to the Father in perfect obedience to God's will, and in atonement for the sins of the world." This profound offering of Mary's, wherein she offered "her own motherly compassion, rights, and suffering...merited more graces than any other created person" (Miravalle, 69). Vatican II speaks on this point: "Thus the Blessed Virgin advanced in her pilgrimage of faith, and faithfully persevered in her union with her Son unto the cross, where she stood, in keeping with the divine plan, enduring with her only begotten Son the intensity of His suffering, associating herself with his sacrifice in her mother's heart, and lovingly consenting to the immolation of this victim which was born of her" (*Lumen Gentium*, No. 58). How appropriate that Jesus should officially designate Mary as our Mother on Calvary, where she, in a totally unique and intense way, participated with him in the meriting of grace - life - for the human family.

C. MEDIATRIX OF ALL GRACE

Motherhood does not stop with the definitive act of giving birth, however, but continues in the nurturing and nourishing of children after birth. The doctrine of Mary as Mediatrix of all grace teaches that all grace that comes to us from God comes through the willed intercession of Mary. Thus, Mary's role as Spiritual Mother is brought to fruition in the nourishing act of mediation. Moreover, it is fitting that Mary nourish her children with the grace that she participated in meriting for them. Her mediation, then, follows from her role as Co-redemptrix, and completes her role as Spiritual Mother.

1. Papal and Magisterial Teachings on Mary as Mediatrix

We find great consistency in the Papal and Magisterial teachings on Mary as Mediatrix. What follows is a list of particularly significant papal / Magisterial pronouncements concerning this issue: Pius VII called Mary the "Dispensatrix of all graces;" Pius IX stated in *Ubi primum* that "...God has committed to Mary the treasury of all good things, in order that everyone may know that through her are obtained every hope, every grace, and all salvation;" Leo XIII referred to her as the "dispenser of all heavenly graces," and stated the following in *Octobri mense*: "With equal truth can it be affirmed that, by the will of God, nothing of the immense treasure of every grace which the Lord has accumulated, comes to us except through Mary...;" St. Pius X. called her "the dispenser of all gifts;" Benedict XV stated, "...we must recognize the mediation of Mary, through whom, according to God's will, every grace and blessing comes to us...;" Pius XI declared, "We have nothing more at heart than to promote more and more the piety of the Christian toward the virgin treasurer of all graces at the side of God;" Vatican Council II referred to Mary as "Mediatrix;" John Paul II devoted the entire third chapter of his encyclical letter Redemptoris Mater to Mary's "maternal mediation." Furthermore, throughout his papacy, John Paul II spoke and wrote consistently and repeatedly of Mary's universal mediation. Such teachings have additionally been echoed in the writings of Benedict XVI (Miravalle, 75-80).

2. Two Conclusions

This impressive display of consistency and repetition in the papal teachings of the ordinary magisterial leads us to draw two theological conclusions: "First, the doctrine of Mary as Mediatrix of all graces must receive from the faithful 'loyal submission of the will and intellect,' which 'must be given, in a special way, to the authentic teaching authority of the Roman Pontiff, even when he does not speak ex cathedra'.... Secondly, in light of the fact that the doctrine of Mary as Mediatrix of all graces has been universally taught throughout the Church by popes of the last 200 years and by bishops in union with them, and in virtue of this universal teaching of the Church, the doctrine of Mediatrix of all graces already possesses the nature of a defined doctrine of the faith" (Miravalle, 80).

D. MEDIATRIX AND CONSECRATION

Having established the irrefutable validity of Mary's role as Mediatrix of all graces, we can now understand the reason for entrusting ourselves to her, which is the essence of Marian consecration. For, how can a mother nourish a child who puts up resistance to her? The more perfectly entrusted to her we are, the more docile we are in her hands, the more perfectly can she nourish us with the milk of divine grace. St. Maximillian Kolbe states, "How can we dispose ourselves so as to receive the greatest possible influx of grace? Let us consecrate ourselves to the Immaculata....This is the most perfect means, the one Jesus prefers, and the one that will afford us the most abundant fruits of grace" (Manteau-Bonamy, 108). Mary, then, is most able to carry out her role as Mediatrix of all with respect to those who have fully entrusted themselves to her via a solemn consecration.

10. TO JESUS THROUGH MARY

Let us now focus on consecration as such, following the path set by St. Louis De Montfort in his famed Treatise on True Devotion to Mary. We shall examine both the nature of and motives for total consecration to Jesus through Mary as presented by the saint.

A. NATURE OF CONSECRATION TO JESUS THROUGH MARY

1. To be 'Hers' is to perfectly be 'His'

De Montfort begins his explanation of the nature of perfect consecration to Jesus through Mary with the following words: "All our perfection consists in being conformed, united, and consecrated to Jesus Christ; and therefore the most perfect of all devotions is, without any doubt, that which the most perfectly conforms, unites, and consecrates us to Jesus Christ. Now, Mary, being the most conformed of all creatures to Jesus Christ, it follows that, of all devotions, that which most consecrates and conforms the soul to our Lord is devotion to his holy mother, and that the more a soul is consecrated to Mary, the more it is consecrated to Jesus... .Hence it comes to pass that the most perfect consecration to Jesus Christ is nothing else but a perfect and entire consecration of ourselves to the Blessed Virgin..." (De Montfort, 77).

The key idea here is that the more perfectly we are consecrated to Mary, the more perfectly will we be consecrated to Jesus. Jesus is the last end of all true devotion to Mary. And the saint makes it clear that devotion to Mary is the most perfect means to the end of transforming union with Christ. Therefore, there can be no limitation to the degree of our belonging to Mary; for the more we are hers, the more perfectly we are His. Many, however, see devotion to Mary as more of an obstacle than a help to our union with Christ. They feel that the more of themselves they give to Mary, the less they have to give to Christ, as if Mary were the last end, keeping for herself whatever we give to her. De Montfort makes clear this point: "She presents these good works to Christ; for she keeps nothing of what is given her for herself, as if she were our last end. She faithfully passes it all onto Jesus. If we give to her, we give necessarily to Jesus" (De Montfort, 93-94).

2. How to be 'Hers' - Formula for Consecration

We must, then, belong entirely to Mary in order to perfectly belong entirely to Jesus. As the saint says, "We must give her (1) our body, with all its senses and members; (2) our soul, with all its powers; (3) our exterior goods of fortune, whether present or to come; (4) our interior or spiritual goods, which are our merits and our virtues, and our good works, past, present, and future" (De Montfort, 78). The saint points out that through this devotion, we give to God through Mary even more than we would through the religious vows of poverty, chastity, and obedience; for in the latter, we do not yet surrender "that which is dearest and most precious, namely, our merits and our satisfactions" (De Montfort, 79).

In virtue of our baptism, we have the right of applying the satisfactory value of our good works to whomsoever we choose, either to ourselves or others. But through the consecration, we surrender this right to Mary. Instead of being detrimental, Miravalle explains how this is supremely beneficial to the mystical body: "Another spiritual effect of this Marian consecration allows for Mary as Mediatrix of all graces and Mother of the Mystical Body to distribute a person's offerings and merits so as to benefit best the body of Christ. The distribution of spiritual benefits is not from our limited earthly perspective, but from the perspective of the Mother of Jesus who is Mother of the Mystical Body" (Miravalle, 113)

3. Renewal of Baptismal Vows
The second essential character of De Montfort's formula for consecration is its "perfect renewal of the vows of holy Baptism" in Mary's hands. His formula begins thus: "I, (name), a faithless sinner, renew and ratify today, in thy hands, O Immaculate Mother, the vows of my Baptism. I renounce forever Satan, his pomp and works, and I give myself entirely to Jesus Christ, the incarnate Wisdom, to carry my cross after him all the days of my life and to be more faithful to him than I have ever been before..." De Montfort makes four important points about this particular renewal of the baptismal vows. First, usually the sacrament of baptism is administered in infancy, the vows being made for the infant by a sponsor. Here, the person himself freely renews the vows that were once made for him. Second, in baptism, a person does not explicitly give himself to Jesus through Mary, which is the perfect way of doing so. Third, in baptism, the person does not give to Jesus and Mary the right of disposing of the satisfactory value of his good works. And finally, the renewal of the baptismal vows makes it that much more difficult to "forget" what we have promised, forgetfulness of these vows being among the major reasons for our continual lapses back into sin (De Montfort, 80-82).

B. MOTIVES
1. It Devotes us to the Service of God
The saint offers eight persuasive motives for the undertaking of this perfect consecration. We will, for the sake of brevity, restrict ourselves to

the first five which, nonetheless, do provide an adequate overview of all the motives. First among them is that "it devotes us entirely to the service of God." In short, everything a soul thus consecrated to Jesus through Mary does, be it great or small, is "done for Jesus and Mary," in virtue of the unlimited and all encompassing character of our offering. We can say in truth and with confidence that we are always and everywhere at the service of Jesus and Mary.

2. An Imitation of Christ and the Trinity
The second motive is a very important one: "it makes us imitate the example of Jesus Christ and of the Holy Trinity and practice humility." As Christians, Christ is our supreme model and exemplar in all things, in all his life. This being so, we see the fittingness of imitating our savior who, becoming a little child, entrusted himself unreservedly to the care of His mother, being docile and allowing himself to be born of and nourished by her. De Montfort stresses this point: "Having, then, before our eyes an example so plain and so well known to the whole world, are we so senseless as to imagine that we can find a more perfect or a shorter means of glorifying God than that of submitting ourselves to Mary after the example of her Son?" (De Montfort, 89).

The saint continues on to explain the dependence that both God the Father and God the Holy Spirit had and have on her; the Father being dependent on her 'fiat' in the conception of the God-Man, and the Holy Spirit likewise being dependent on her 'fiat' in the distribution of every grace that comes to us by Him. "After so many and such pressing examples of the Most Holy Trinity, can we without extreme blindness dispense with Mary, can we fail to consecrate ourselves to her for the purpose of going to God and sacrificing ourselves to God?" (De Montfort, 89). Furthermore, as the saint puts it, "this devotion is a practice of great humility, which God loves above all the other virtues" (De Montfort, 91). And this is because we are not so bold and self assured as to approach our Lord Jesus Christ without the assistance of a mediator, in fact, the very same medium by which he chose to come to us - His and our most holy Mother Mary.

3. Obtains for us the Good Offices of Mary
The third motive is that "it obtains for us the good offices of the Blessed Virgin" (De Montfort, 91). First, the saint explains that Mary, "who never lets herself be outdone in love and liberality, seeing that we give ourselves entirely to her, to honor and to serve her, and for that end strip ourselves of all that is dearest to us, in order to adorn her, meets us in the same spirit" (De Montfort, 91). This is a key point to the understanding of

living in union with the two Hearts of Jesus and Mary. Mary, seeing that we have given ourselves unreservedly to her, likewise gives herself entirely to us, adorning us with the plenitude of her graces and virtues. Just as what is ours, through consecration, becomes hers, so too does what is hers truly become ours. Speaking on this, the saint states, "She also gives her whole self, and gives it in an unspeakable manner, to him who gives all to her. She causes him to be engulfed in the abyss of her graces. She adorns him with her merits; she supports him with her power; she illuminates him with her light; she inflames him with her love; she communicates to him her virtues: her humility, her faith, her purity, and the rest" (De Montfort, 91-92).

Thus, we see how consecration to Mary most perfectly unites us to Christ; for Mary's heart becomes ours to adore Christ with. We adore Christ with the most perfect and pure love of the Immaculate Heart of Mary; we contemplate His real presence in the Eucharist with the pure light of Mary's faith; we hope in the divine Mercy and the Providence of the Father with the very certainty of Mary's hope. A second aspect of this third motive is equally as amazing; Mary truly purifies, embellishes, and makes acceptable to her Son every gift we give to Him through her. Being in the fallen state that we are, even the best of our good works are usually not without some "stain of self love." De Montfort, speaking on our good works states: "As soon as they are in her pure and fruitful hands, those same hands which have never been sullied or idle and which purify whatever they touch, take away from the present which we give her all that was spoiled or imperfect about it"{ (De Montfort, 93). What is more, "she embellishes our works, adorning them with her own merits and virtues" (De Montfort, 93). He presents the analogy of a peasant who desires to give to his king a gift of an apple, which is all the peasant has to give. By itself, the apple is not a fitting gift for a king. But if the peasant were to give this apple to the Queen, who would then peel and artfully carve, slice and garnish it, and then place it on a gold platter and herself present it to the King, no doubt it would be well received. In like manner are our gifts purified, embellished, and made acceptable to God by the Queen of heaven and earth.

4. The Greater Glory of God

The fourth motive that De Montfort offers is that "it is an excellent means of procuring God's greater glory" (De Montfort, 95). We are all obliged to labor for the greater glory of God, but scarcely do we attain to this noble end. Either we don't desire to do so, or we don't know where it is to be found. Mary, on the other hand, knows perfectly, and by entrusting to her all our merits and good works, we enable her to employ them to the fullest extent for God's greatest glory.

5. An Easy, Short, Perfect, and Secure Way to Jesus

We find in the fifth motive profound insights into this Marian spirituality, particularly as it pertains to the interior life. The saint claims that this devotion of total consecration to Mary "is an easy, short, perfect and secure way of attaining union with our Lord, in which union the perfection of a Christian consists" (De Montfort, 96). How is it that this is an 'easy' way? In this fascinating section, De Montfort explains that it is true that there are other roads by which to reach transforming union with Christ, but that these roads are much more difficult. In his own words: It is an easy way. It is the way which Jesus Christ Himself trod in coming to us, and in which there is no obstacle in reaching Him. It is true that we can attain divine union by other roads; but it is by many more crosses and strange deaths, and with many more difficulties which we shall find it hard to overcome. We must pass through obscure nights, through combats, through strange agonies, over craggy mountains, through cruel thorns and over frightful deserts. But by the path of Mary we pass more gently and more tranquilly" (De Montfort, 96).

Could the "obscure nights" he speaks of here be referring to the same "dark nights" experienced by such great mystics as John of the Cross and the Little Flower? Is it possible that this Marian path makes 'detours' around such dark nights? But he later goes on to say that 'easier doesn't necessarily mean fewer crosses and less suffering. In fact, it is often the case that these faithful clients of Mary experience greater sufferings, as this good mother wants nothing more than to transform the soul into a faithful replica of Christ crucified. So how is this easier? De Montfort answers: "That good Mother, all full of grace and of the unction of the Holy Spirit prepares her servant's crosses with so much maternal sweetness and pure love as to make them gladly acceptable, no matter how bitter they may be in themselves."

Further on, he calls devotion to Mary "the sweetmeat and confection of crosses" (De Montfort, 97-98). Mary, desiring our greatest possible sanctification, will necessarily provide more opportunities and occasions for suffering, for it is precisely in suffering that we are conformed to her crucified Son. But she will do so in the sweetest possible manner; her heart will become a refuge in which her suffering clients will receive heavenly consolations reserved exclusively for such as them. And experiencing the goodness of this Mother, and the joys of paradise in her heart, these suffering servants will be entirely renewed and embrace their crosses all the more lovingly and joyfully. Secondly, De Montfort claims that this is a short way – "both because it is a road from which we do not stray, and because, as I have just said, it is a road we tread with joy and facility, and consequently with promptitude."

With Mary, we make strides in the spiritual life. First, it is difficult to stray from this road, for we are being guided and supported by Mary. Second, since we follow this path with "joy and facility," we will necessarily reach our goal more quickly. Hence, this is a short way. Thirdly, this road to Jesus is a perfect one; first because Mary herself is the most perfect of all creatures, and secondly, because it was this way, and no other way, that Jesus chose in coming to us. If Christ Himself, the eternal Word of God, chose no other way than Mary in coming to us, would it not be presumptuous, arrogant, and foolish to think there exists a better or more perfect way of returning to Him?

To stress this point, De Montfort makes the following remarks: "Make for me, if you will, a new road to go to Jesus, and pave it with all the merits of the Blessed, adorn it with all their heroic virtues, illuminate and embellish it with all the lights and beauties of the angels, and let all the angels and saints be there themselves to escort, defend, and sustain those who are ready to walk there; and yet in truth, in simple truth, I say boldly, and I repeat that I say truly, I would prefer to this new, perfect path the immaculate way of Mary" (De Montfort, 100). Finally, the saint assures us that his path to Jesus through Mary is a secure way. First, it is secure in the sense of its rootedness in Tradition. Records available to De Montfort at that time suggested that, at least in France, this devotion had been publicly practiced since 1040 AD. But, as Miravalle points out, the essence of this devotion can be traced as far back as the fifth and sixth centuries (Miravalle, 109). Furthermore, Pope John Paul the Great assures us of the "security" of this way in his encyclical, *Redemptoris Mater,* wherein he states, "Furthermore, Marian spirituality, like its corresponding devotion, finds a very rich source in the historical experience of individuals and of the various Christian communities present among the different peoples and nations of the world. In this regard, I would like to recall, among the many witnesses and teachers of this spirituality, the figure of Saint Louis Marie Grignion de Montfort, who proposes consecration to Christ through the hands of Mary as an effective means for Christians to live faithfully their baptismal commitments" (*Redemptoris Mater,* Para 48).

Second, it is secure in the sense that it is truly impossible for Mary to do anything other than lead souls to Jesus Christ. Mary, whose will is utterly conformed to the divine will, desires nothing but, and works exclusively for, the accomplishment of that divine will. But we can still ask whether it is ever possible for Mary to be a hindrance to our union with God. In response to this question, the saint replies with the following: "It is quite true that the view of other creatures, however holy, may perhaps at certain times retard divine union. But this cannot be said of Mary, as I have remarked before, and shall never weary of repeating....Thus, so far from the divine Mary, all absorbed in God, being an obstacle to the perfect in attaining union with God, there has never been up to this time, and there never will be, any creature who will aid us more efficaciously in this great work" (de Montfort, 105).

11.   IN THE SPIRIT OF ST. JOSEPH

Having explored both the theological foundations of consecration to Jesus through Mary, as well as its essence and motives as presented by St. Louis de Montfort, let us now turn our attention to St. Joseph and his unique role in this devotion. John Paul II states in his Apostolic Exhortation *Redemptoris Gustos;* "Besides trusting in Joseph's sure protection, the Church also trusts in his noble example, which transcends all individual states of life and serves as a model for the entire Christian community, whatever the condition and duties of each of its members may be" (*Redemptoris Gustos,* Para. 30). Thus, this section will be divided into three parts. First, we will present Joseph as the supreme "example," or model of total consecration to Jesus through Mary. Second, we will examine his role as "protector," or spiritual father of the mystical body. Finally, we will focus on how Joseph becomes a model for all, particularly the laity.

A. JOSEPH AS SUPREME MODEL OF UNION WITH THE TWO HEARTS

Tradition has consistently regarded Joseph as among the highest in virtue of all the saints. This has much to do with the reality of his constant association with and solicitousness for Jesus and Mary. Yet we know very little about the life of this great protector of and provider for the Holy Family. Let us, then, explore the dynamic nature of St. Joseph's sanctity, specifically as it pertains to his wholly unique relationship with the Two Hearts of Jesus and Mary.

1. Joseph's Spousal Union with Mary Epitomizes Consecration to Her

We have already explained how total consecration to Mary is the most perfect way to union with Christ. The more perfectly we live in union with Mary, the more perfectly will we be united to Christ. The essence of consecration to Mary consists in the giving of our hearts ("heart" meaning the very totality of our being) to her. We also discussed how she in turn meets us in the same spirit, giving to us her heart. There is here an exchange of hearts; the two become so utterly united as to become one. Now, if we take this understanding of total consecration and compare it to St. Joseph's spousal relationship to Mary, we can see how his union with her epitomizes total consecration to Mary. For, in his espousal of her, he gave his heart unreservedly to her and took her heart as his own. The hearts of Joseph and Mary became one; through the marital union, they became as "two in one flesh." Thus, Joseph was necessarily united to the Heart of Christ, since the Immaculate heart of Mary and the Sacred Heart of Jesus are inseparably united. Reverend Stanley Smolensk, contemporary Josephologist, explains this point: "[Joseph's] interior life was based on his singular union with Jesus through Mary. He was consecrated to Jesus through Mary by his espousal to her.... Thus Joseph's consecration is the epitome of all consecrations to Jesus through Mary" (Smolenski, 3). Thus, we can understand Joseph's sanctity as the fruit of his union with the two hearts, based on his espousal union with the heart of Mary. And we too can model our total consecration to Jesus through Mary on St. Joseph's "spousal" union with Mary. We, like Joseph, are called to "espouse" the Immaculate Heart of Mary; to give Mary our hearts undividedly and take her heart as our own.

2. 'Spouse' as Compared to 'Slave,' 'Possession and Property'

Throughout the history of Marian consecration, there have been many different but complementary ways of describing the totality of the entrustment. St. Louis de Montfort was fond of the term "slave;" this, he believed, sufficiently expressed the unreserved nature of the consecration. St. Maximillian Kolbe, however, felt that even this term didn't go far enough. Instead, he advocated the terms "possession and property." But both of these great Marian saints fully agreed that to live this consecration was to live "with Mary, in Mary, through Mary, and for Mary" (Denis, 35).

In short, to live with Mary is to take Mary as the model of all that we do; to live in Mary is to say that "Mary will be the only means used by our soul in dealing with God; she will be our universal refuge;" to live through Mary is to never go to God without her; and to live for her is to make her the proximate end of all our actions (Denis, 38). Yet, does not the model of "espousal" seem to most completely embody and connote the charism of living with, through, in, and for Mary? St. Joseph's spousal union with Mary, then, epitomizes total consecration to her and serves as the perfect model for our union with the two hearts. Speaking on this, contemporary spiritual writer Aaron Joseph states the following: "in imitation of St. Joseph, we too can...espouse [Mary's] heart, becoming "two in one flesh"(Gen. 2:24), in living with Jesus, loving God and neighbor. This way of St. Joseph can be seen in the imagery of old Jerusalem. As the temple of the Lord stood in the heart of this city of David, Jerusalem, containing the Holy of Holies, in a similar way, in the heart of Joseph, son of David (Mt. 1:20), through his spousal relationship with Mary, stands this Immaculate Temple of the Lord, whose heart contains the Spirit and the Light of Christ. Thus, Joseph, in his spousal relationship with Jesus through Mary, becomes...a model for the Church" (Joseph, 12).

3. Scriptural Basis for the Espousal Model

He goes on to offer solid scriptural grounding for the universality of the "espousal" model of consecration to the Immaculate Heart of Mary. In Eccl.15:1-2, we read, "He that fears God will do good, and he that possesses justice shall lay hold on her (Wisdom/Mary) and she will meet him as an honorable mother, and will receive him as a wife married of a virgin." Likewise, in Wisdom 8:2, "Her have I loved, and have sought her out from my youth, and have desired to take her for my spouse, and I became a lover of her beauty." In both these passages, the "her" refers to personified Wisdom which the Church, in her Liturgy, interprets as representing Mary.

4. Espousal and Spiritual Motherhood

We must be careful here, though, to not make the mistake of thinking that this espousal model does away with or replaces Mary's role as Spiritual Mother. On the contrary, the espousal model compliments Mary's Spiritual Motherhood; for it is by our espousal of Mary's Heart that Mary is most able to act as our Mother. As we saw earlier, consecration to Mary enables Mary to most fully carry out her role as Mediatrix of all graces. If this is true, then it follows that "espousal," being the most perfect form of consecration, allows Mary to provide for us as Mother in the most perfect and complete manner.

B. JOSEPH AS SPIRITUAL FATHER OF THE MYSTICAL BODY

A second dimension to Joseph's role in this devotion is his spiritual fatherhood of the Mystical Body, the Church. Smolenski explains this point: "He is the virginal father of Jesus. But just as Mary is the Mother not only of Jesus, but of His Mystical Body, the Church, as well, so Joseph is, in a relative way, the spiritual father of the Mystical Body, the Church, as well" (Smolenski, 2).

1. Dispenser of the Treasures of the Sacred Heart

How is it that Joseph provides for the Church as spiritual father? Blessed Brother Andre Bassett, known for his great devotion to the patriarch of Nazareth, held the following: "If Jesus remains the sole sanctifier, the never failing source of all graces; if the Blessed Virgin, who came nearest to this supernatural source, being the Mediatrix of all grace, turns the course of that stream towards the earth, then St. Joseph as the protector of the Church is the steward who distributes the divine favors to men" (Bergeron, 123). The Little Flower, St. Therese of Lisieux, similarly had recourse to Joseph as the "dispenser of the treasures of [Christ's] Sacred Heart." Like Mary, whose role as Spiritual Mother is brought to fruition in the mediation of all grace to her children, Joseph's role as spiritual father is likewise carried out through the mediation or distribution of grace. And we must acknowledge that his mediation is, in a certain sense, universal - that is, his intercessory power extends at least over all necessities and persons.

De Domenico states the following concerning the universality of Joseph's mediation: "But the mediation of St. Joseph is something more than being more powerful than all the other saints except Our Lady. It is distinctly universal. The word universal implies "all" in some way" (De Domenico, 98). But does this universal mediation of Joseph pertain to all graces as well? Although the magesterium has made no official pronouncement on the matter, many theologians present evidence pointing to the affirmative. De Domenico, in his book, *True Devotion to St. Joseph and the Church*, offers seven proofs for Joseph as mediator of all grace after Mary. But regardless of whether or not Joseph mediates all graces to humanity after Mary, the fact of the unique universality of his mediation as Patron of the Universal Church remains undisputed. And this alone provides a firm foundation for recourse to Joseph as Spiritual Father.

2. The Terrestrial Trinity

At this point, we begin to see how true devotion to St. Joseph, with an understanding of his roles as supreme model for consecration and spiritual father of the mystical body, completes, as it were, true devotion to Jesus through Mary. With Joseph, the picture is complete - the Holy Family is no longer Jesus and Mary, with Joseph haphazardly on the scene. Rather, Joseph's presence is a necessary presence - necessary for us. He provides the example of one who lives in perfect union with Jesus through Mary. Further, he continues his providential function as spiritual father, assisting us through his intercession to live his union with the two hearts. The Holy Family, then, is composed of three distinct persons who are, nonetheless, truly one in love. How appropriate were the words of St. Francis de Sales on this, who stated, "We may say the Holy Family was a Trinity on earth, which in a certain way represented the Heavenly Trinity Itself" (Thompson, 12).

C. A Spirituality for the Laity

Finally, Joseph is a model of holiness for all, particularly the laity. As we previously noted, John Paul II points out that Joseph's example "transcends all individual states of life and serves as a model for the entire Christian community, whatever the condition and duties of each of its members may be." Chapter five of *Lumen Gentium* makes clear that all persons, without exception, are called to Christian perfection. Smolenski explains how this universal call to holiness requires the universal spirituality that the Holy Family, the terrestrial trinity, offers: "Today the laity stands with the clergy and religious in the shared responsibility of the Church for evangelization and sanctification of the entire world. This requires a universal spirituality to direct to that goal. Because this call to holiness is universal, the foundation of this spirituality must be universal: the universality of Jesus, Mary, and Joseph" (Smolenski, 1).

Conclusion

Thus, we have presented a profoundly sanctifying devotion; a perfect devotion to Jesus, through Mary, in the spirit of St. Joseph. We began with an explanation of Mary's role as Mediatrix of all graces as the firm theological groundwork for Marian consecration. Then we explored the essence and motives of this consecration as explained by St. Louis de Montfort. Finally, we concluded by looking to St. Joseph's role in this devotion, showing how true devotion to him, with an understanding of his roles as model and spiritual father, completes true devotion to Jesus through Mary, and provides the foundation for a spirituality that is truly universal in its scope. Let us hasten, then, towards an intimate union with Jesus, through Mary, in the spirit of St. Joseph. We close with the following words of John Paul II: "Following St. Joseph's example, may all believers achieve in their own life a deep harmony between prayer and work, between meditation on the word of God and their daily occupations. May an intimate and vital relationship with Jesus, the Incarnate Word, and His Holy Mother always be at the heart of everything" (John Paul, March 20, 1996).

12.   LIVING THE CONSECRATION

Essays on Essential Marian/Eucharistic Devotions and Practices

Our Lady of Medjugorje (currently under investigation by the Vatican and not by the local ordinary) calls for deep, profound conversion of the world back to God. Anyone who has read any of the messages knows that they are intended for everyone; for persons from all walks of life, ethnicities, cultures, and educational backgrounds. Thus, the messages are quite simple and to the point, as compared to the theologically rich messages given via interior locution to Fr. Gobbi of the Marian Movement of Priests. In keeping with the simplicity of the messages of Medjugorje, what this author refers to as the "Fatima of our times", the over-arching message or plan of action, as dictated by Our Lady to the seers, has been encapsulated into a formula of life sometimes referred to as the Five Stones. Simply, the Five Stones, listed on the back of most "Our Lady of Medjugorje" prayer cards, are (1) prayer from the heart, especially the Holy Rosary (2) Participation in the Holy Sacrifice of the Mass and reception of the Eucharist (3) Monthly Confession (4) Reading of the Scripture (5) a return to the practice of fasting on bread and water on Wednesdays and Fridays.

Part III of this book is devoted to explaining the three most important of these "5 Stones" that (1) lay the foundation for a practical spirituality that can be had by anyone and everyone, and (2) additionally lie at the heart of living one's total consecration to Mary. The Chapters will proceed according to the following outline: (1) The Eucharist; (2) To Forgive and be Forgiven – The Sacrament of Reconciliation; (3) The Most Holy Rosary; and (4) God's Message of Mercy to the World through St. Faustina.

Daily Reception of the Eucharist: The Central Sacrament

Christ's institution of the sacrament of the Eucharist was and is the single greatest gift He left to His Church. For, it is the fulfillment of His promise to truly be always among us, as he states in Matthew 28:20, "And know that I am with you always; yes, to the end of time." While there are, indeed, multiple and varied presences of Christ, such as when two or three are gathered in His name, when the People of God gather to celebrate the Liturgy, when Sacred Scripture – the Word – is proclaimed, or when the priest acts in Persona Christi while administering and/or officiating at any of the sacraments, etc., the abiding Eucharistic presence of Christ, with the fullness of His Body, Blood, Soul and Divinity is truly singular in its reality, intensity, substance and fullness. While the accidents of bread and wine remain, the substance is completely transformed into the Second Person of the Trinity.

This process whereby bread and wine are transformed into the true presence, flesh and blood of Christ is referred to as transubstantiation. This occurs during the second half of the Sacred Liturgy, or the Liturgy of the Eucharist, specifically during the priest's prayer of consecration and immediately following the Epiclesis. Regarding the wholly unique presence of Christ contained within the pre-eminent sacrament of the Holy Eucharist, the Catechism of the Catholic Church has this to say: "The mode of Christ's presence under the Eucharistic species is unique. It raises the Eucharist above all the sacraments as 'the perfection of the spiritual life and the end to which all sacraments tend.' In the most blessed sacrament of the Eucharist 'the body and blood, together with the soul and divinity, of our Lord Jesus Christ and, therefore, *the whole Christ is truly, really, and substantially* contained.' 'This presence is called 'real' – by which is not intended to exclude the other types of presence as if they could not be 'real' too, but because it is presence in the fullest sense: that is to say, it is a *substantial* presence by which Christ, God and man, makes himself wholly and entirely present.'" (CCC, 1374).

Lumen Gentium, the Second Vatican Council's Dogmatic Constitution on the Church, refers to the Eucharist as the source from which all the Church's activity originates and the summit toward which all the Church's activity is directed. Based on this essential teaching of the Council, which reiterated 2000 years of Church teaching on the Eucharist, we can come to understand that the Eucharist truly is the "central Sacrament" in the sense that the Eucharist is "the end to which all sacraments tend." Stated clearly in the paragraph quoted above, this truth fleshes out the reality that each of the other Sacraments, while possessing a specific purpose in their own right, ultimately serve the greater purpose of leading souls to full participation in the Eucharistic banquet, which is nothing short of a foretaste of the heavenly banquet, where we will participate in God's own divine life. For example, while the sacrament of Baptism has the specific purpose of forgiving original sin and imparting sanctifying grace, its greater purpose is to allow the Baptized to fully partake of the Eucharistic banquet; for, unless one is Baptized, he or she cannot fully participate in the Liturgy of the Eucharist and be nourished with Christ's body and blood. Moreover, it is essential that we be nourished with this "bread from heaven," for, as Christ Himself states, "I tell you most solemnly, if you do not eat the flesh of the Son of Man and drink His blood, you will not have life in you" (John, 6:53).

Just as it is with Baptism, so is it with all the remaining sacraments: reconciliation makes it possible for us to return to the Eucharist after we have fallen; Confirmation imparts the seven-fold gifts of the Spirit to better prepare us to enter into the mystery of the Eucharistic Pasch; Matrimony is used by Christ to pre-figure the great wedding-feast of the Lamb, with Christ as the Bridegroom, and His Mystical Body, the Church, as His Bride; clearly, the sacrament of Holy Orders is primary concerned with imparting sacramental "character" on the priest's soul, thereby enabling him to act in Persona Christi for the sake of celebrating the Holy Sacrifice of the Mass, where, of course, the Eucharist is made present and with which the Baptized are spiritually nourished; and finally, the Anointing of the Sick, of which reception of the Eucharist, or viaticum (bread for the journey) is an integral part, and the Anointing itself being given ultimately for the sake of spiritual healing, which is necessary to partake of the Eucharist. Thus, it is quite clear that each of the Sacraments has, as its ultimate end, the facilitation of participation in the Eucharistic banquet.

As an aside, I find it most curious that many Protestant groups, especially fundamentalists, who tend to interpret almost all of Scripture in a most literal fashion, stop short of a literal interpretation of Christ's teachings on the Eucharist, which they strangely regard as merely symbolic. Let us turn to Scripture itself to read with our own eyes just what Christ stated regarding the Eucharist. Beginning in John, 6:48 and following, Jesus states the following: "I am the bread of life. Your fathers ate the manna in the wilderness, and they died. This is the bread which comes down from heaven, that a man may eat of it and not die. I am the living bread which came down from heaven; if anyone eats of this bread, he will live forever; and the bread which I shall give is my flesh for the life of the world.... Truly, truly, I say to you, unless you eat the flesh of the Son of man and drink his blood, you have no life in you; he who eats my flesh and drinks my blood has eternal life, and I will raise him up on the last day. For my flesh is food indeed, and my blood is drink indeed. He who eats my flesh and drinks my blood abides in me, and I in him."

And then again, in Matthew, 26:26 and following, this is reported: "Now on the night he was betrayed, the Lord Jesus took some bread, and when he had said the blessing he broke it. And he gave it to the disciples, saying, 'Take it and eat. This is my body.' Then he took a cup, and when he had given thanks he gave it to them. 'Drink all of you from this,' he said. 'For this is my blood, the blood of the new covenant, which is to be poured out for many for the forgiveness of sins.'" If fundamentalist Protestant Christians tend to interpret almost everything in Scripture literally, then why not these words of Christ?

Having addressed that issue, let us now discuss the marvelous effects of a well received Holy Communion. The Catechism of the Catholic Church states that "The principle fruit of receiving the Eucharist in Holy Communion is an intimate union with Christ Jesus" (CCC, 1391). Moreover, Holy Communion "preserves increases and renews the life of grace received at Baptism" (CCC, 1391). Thus, this Living Bread come down from Heaven truly nourishes the divine life in our souls. Just as the body needs material food to be nourished, strengthened and rejuvenated, so too does our soul need the spiritual food of the Eucharist to nourish, strengthen, enliven and rejuvenate the divine life that is the soul of our soul.

Secondly, "the Eucharist cannot unite us to Christ without at the same time cleansing us from past sins and preserving us from future sins" (CCC, 1393). Reception of this sacrament increases our charity and forgives us our venial sins. Simultaneously, in strengthening our charity, it facilitates our bond with Christ and makes it that much more difficult to extinguish the divine life within us through commission of mortal sin. Although Holy Communion does, in fact, forgive us our venial sins, we are not permitted to receive this sacrament if we have fallen into mortal sin, as the Eucharist is the sacrament of the living, or those in full communion with the Mystical Body – the Church. Forgiveness of mortal sins properly takes place within the context of the sacrament of Reconciliation. What is more, the Eucharist builds up the Church, the Mystical Body of Christ, by uniting us through the bond of charity with Christ, the Head of the Body, and with the members of his Body. The Eucharist is the fulfillment of the Baptismal grace, which unites and conjoins us to the Church: "Because there is one bread, we who are many are one body, for we all partake of the one bread" (1 Cor 10:16-17).

The Eucharist is also "A pledge of future glory." An ancient prayer of the Church provides a catechetical summary of the Eucharist and reads as follows: "O Sacred Banquet, in which Christ is received, the memory of

His passion is renewed, the soul is filled with grace, and a pledge of future glory is given to us." It would behoove us to commit this prayerful ejaculation to memory, as it wonderfully and simply sums up the most salient catechetical tenets concerning the Eucharistic doctrine. We are, however, chiefly concerned here with the final thought contained in this prayer. For, Christ pledges to "raise up on the last day" those who "eat the flesh of the Son of man and drink his blood." The Sacred Liturgy is an earthly foretaste of the heavenly Banquet, the wedding feast of the Lamb spoken of in the book of Revelation. Thus, the coming of Christ in the Eucharist takes on an eschatological significance, as each Eucharistic celebration pre-figures the second coming of Christ, that eschatological reality for which the human heart ardently longs as we pray, with the Church: Maranatha! – Come, Lord Jesus!

Finally, because Jesus is truly present in an abiding fashion with His body, blood, soul and divinity in the Eucharistic species of bread and wine, it is laudable to practice devotion to His Eucharistic presence in the consecrated and reserved host. A consecrated host should be placed in a monstrance, which should then be placed on the altar, preferably surrounded by candles and flowers, in order that the faithful might practice the pious devotion of Eucharistic Adoration. While it is theologically correct to say that the Eucharist is primarily meant to be consumed by Catholic Christians in a state of grace, solemn veneration of the Eucharist exposed is a most salutary and pious practice that evolved over time and has been encouraged by popes, saints and doctors of the Church. Eucharistic adoration can be seen as a response to Christ's call to His disciples to "keep watch with [him] for one hour" (Matt 26:40). Hence, the origins of the practice of the Eucharistic Holy Hour.

Jesus the Passover Lamb of Sacrifice

At the last supper, the single most important passover meal ever celebrated, Christ manifests His identity as the passover lamb of sacrifice. In the Old Testament, during the very first passover, an innocent, unblemished lamb is sacrificed. The blood of the sacrificed lamb is placed on the doorposts of the Israelites houses, to save the firstborn males from death. The lamb, which is slain as a sacrifice to the Father, is then consumed by the Israelites to strengthen them for their journey through the desert, toward the promised land. Moreover, as the Jews wander throughout the desert, they are fed with manna, a bread from heaven, which is divinely given to them by God on a daily basis. In the New Testament, Jesus is the unblemished Lamb of God who offers himself as a sacrifice of atonement to the Father, thereby saving us from the death of sin and hell. It is precisely his blood that saves us from spiritual death. Moreover, Jesus offers us his own body, which has just been sacrificed, to spiritually strengthen us on our journey through the desert of this life as we make our way to the Promised Land of Heaven. Moreover, Jesus is the manna, the "bread from heaven" that we are nourished with on a day-to-day basis, as the Father provides all that we need, not more, not less.

Thus, to truly enter into the mystery of the Eucharistic Pasch, we need to turn our attention to the Old Testament narrative of the very first Passover meal. Only then will we begin to understand, however superficially (after all, this is a mystery of the deposit of faith), the tremendous significance of our Eucharistic Passover meal and sacrifice in the Holy Sacrifice of the Mass, and the grand mystery of Christ's infinite, perfect, merciful and sadly, often unrequited, love for humanity in His real presence in the Eucharist.

13. TO FORGIVE AND BE FORGIVEN

Reconciliation

St. Paul exhorts us to get rid of all envy, jealousy, bitterness and anger. This admonition ought to be taken quite seriously, as each of these states is profoundly detrimental to the psychological, spiritual and even physical wellbeing of the human person. The only way to rid ourselves of such negativity, however, is through authentic, sincere forgiveness and prayer. It is only natural, given our fallen state, to experience such negative emotions and sentiments when we have been wronged or when life has seemingly been unfair to us. In order to preserve our psycho-spiritual equilibrium, it is absolutely imperative that we learn to forgive, and leave it to God to bring about justice. As for forgiveness, it must be noted that it is truly an ongoing process, especially when we have been hurt deeply.

For, each time the injustice comes to mind, we must redouble our efforts to forgive from the heart. And it is precisely throughout this process of ongoing forgiveness that our own hearts are softened and, with the passage of time and the action of the Holy Spirit in our souls, the negativity dissipates. We must understand that forgiveness does more for the person who's doing the forgiving than it does for the one being forgiven. Neither must we forget the spiritual axiom that we will only be forgiven by God to the extent that we ourselves forgive others, as is so clearly elucidated in the Lord's Prayer. Yes, forgiveness benefits our psychological, spiritual and physical wellbeing as human persons. Let us, then, ask our Lord to provide us with the graces necessary to forgive at all times, in all circumstances, despite the severity of the wrong that has been done to us. After all, harboring resentment can and will lead to psychological, physical and spiritual illness, and in the most extreme cases, spiritual death.

Moreover, forgiveness is a two-way street. Not only must we forgive those who trespass against us, but we, ourselves, must allow ourselves to experience the forgiveness of God. Catholic teaching on the issue of forgiveness is that if we have committed a serious, mortal sin, that is, having performed an action that is objectively evil and that was committed with full knowledge and full consent of the will, we have the right and the obligation to confess our sin to a validly ordained priest who, acting in Persona Christi, has the power to absolve us of our sins provided we confess all mortal sins that we are aware of, are truly contrite, make a firm resolve to sin no more, and perform the prescribed penance. It would be helpful here to make a distinction between perfect contrition and attrition, or imperfect contrition. Perfect contrition consists of compunction of heart, a detestation of sin, and a firm resolve to sin no more, all springing from a perfect, pure love for God as our greatest good. In cases of perfect contrition, the Church teaches that God will forgive even our mortal sins directly and immediately, provided that we take the opportunity to avail ourselves of the sacrament of penance as soon as a priest or the sacrament is available. Attrition, on the other hand, is an imperfect sorrow for sin that rises out of a concern for the self and a fear of going to hell should we die before going to confession. Attrition is sufficient for forgiveness in the confessional, but is not sufficient for the forgiveness of a mortal sin outside the context of Sacramental Penance.

It is most unfortunate that many Catholics have fallen out of the practice of monthly confession. It seems that psychotherapists have, by and large, taken the place of validly ordained ministers of the soul – priests – and often attempt to ease the burden of guilt by justifying so many immoral actions, viewing the latter as mere idiosyncrasies of behavior rather than morally illicit actions. This is not to dismiss the role of the psychotherapist in assisting individuals who are attempting to deal with real sentiments of guilt and shame. Certainly, psychotherapists have an integral role to play in the restoration of psychological and even spiritual health to their clients. It goes without saying, however, that a therapist is not an ordained minister and has no power to act in the person of Christ or on behalf of the Church in extending true pardon and peace to a contrite soul seeking forgiveness from God, who is the one offended in every sin committed on the part of human persons.

In sum, the key to psycho-spiritual freedom consists in both forgiving from the heart and being forgiven. Christ, in His infinite wisdom, knew the therapeutic, healing power of both the confession of sins to another person acting in His own Divine Person, as well as the healing power of hearing the words of absolution being spoken and granted through the authority of both Christ and His Church. It goes without saying that Christ was and is the King of kings and the Lord of Lords; but in addition to that, he was the greatest psychologist who ever walked the face of the earth. Christ was the "firstborn of all creation, all was created through Him, all was created for Him." Moreover, he forever grafted a true human nature to His Divine Person. In His infinite wisdom, He established a profound sacrament of healing, knowing with a perfect, divine knowledge, what man needed both spiritually and psychologically to both receive and experience the healing power that is transmitted via the profound sacrament of reconciliation. It would be most foolish of us to not take advantage of this tremendous sacrament of forgiveness and healing. If we were as concerned with the cleanliness of our souls as we are with the cleanliness of our bodies, we'd be in the confessional on a daily basis.

Examination of Conscience

In order to make a good confession of our sins, it is necessary that we set aside some quiet time for prayer, reflection and meditation, petitioning the Holy Spirit to enlighten our intellect as we thoughtfully bring to mind all of our serious sins of commission or omission. Many individuals find it helpful to have a guide according to which they may examine their conscience. For the sake of convenience, I have below reproduced a fairly comprehensive guide for the examination of one's conscience based on the Ten Commandments and the Precepts of the Church, quoted from www.beginningCatholic.com:

The Ten Commandments

FIRST COMMANDMENT
I am the LORD your God. You shall worship the Lord your God and Him only shall you serve.
Have I...
- Disobeyed the commandments of God or the Church?
- Refused to accept what God has revealed as true, or what the Catholic Church proposes for belief?
- Denied the existence of God?
- Nourished and protected my faith?
- Rejected everything opposed to a sound faith?
- Deliberately misled others about doctrine or the faith?
- Rejected the Catholic faith, joined another Christian denomination, or joined or practiced another religion?
- Joined a group forbidden to Catholics (Masons, communists, and so on)?
- Despaired about my salvation or the forgiveness of my sins?
- Presumed on God's mercy? (Committing a sin in expectation of forgiveness, or asking for forgiveness without conversion and practicing virtue.)

- Loved someone or something more than God (money, power, sex, ambition, and so on)?
- Let someone or something influence my choices more than God?
- Engaged in superstitious practices? (Incl. horoscopes, fortune tellers, and so on)
- Been involved in the occult? (Séances, Ouija board, worship of Satan, and so on)
- Formally left the Catholic Church?
- Hidden a serious sin or told a lie in confession?

SECOND COMMANDMENT

You shall not take the name of the Lord your God in vain.

Have I...

- Used the name of God in cursing or blasphemy?
- Failed to keep vows or promises that I have made to God?
- Spoken about the Faith, the Church, the saints, or sacred things with irreverence, hatred or defiance?
- Watched television or movies, or listened to music that treated God, the Church, the saints, or sacred things irreverently?
- Used vulgar, suggestive or obscene speech?
- Belittled others in my speech?
- Behaved disrespectfully in Church?
- Misused places or things set apart for the worship of God?
- Committed perjury? (Breaking an oath or lying under oath.)
- Blamed God for my failings?

THIRD COMMANDMENT

Remember to keep holy the Sabbath day.

Have I...

- Set time aside each day for personal prayer to God?
- Missed Mass on Sunday or Holy Days (through own fault w/o sufficient reason)?
- Committed a sacrilege against the Blessed Sacrament?
- Received a sacrament while in the state of mortal sin?
- Habitually come late to and/or leave early from Mass without a good reason?
- Shop, labor, or do business unnecessarily on Sunday or other Holy Days of Obligation?
- Not attend to taking my children to Mass?
- Knowingly eat meat on a forbidden day (or not fasting on a fast day)?
- Eat or drink within one hour of receiving Communion (other than medical need)?

FOURTH COMMANDMENT

Honor your father and your mother.

Have I...

- (If still under my parents' care) Obeyed all that my parents reasonably asked of me?
- Neglected the needs of my parents in their old age or in their time of need?
- (If still in school) Obeyed the reasonable demands of my teachers?
- Neglected to give my children proper food, clothing, shelter, education, discipline and care (even after Confirmation)?
- Provided for the religious education and formation of my children for as long as they are under my care?
- Ensured that my children still under my care regularly frequent the sacraments of Penance and Holy Communion?
- Educated my children in a way that corresponds to my religious convictions?
- Provided my children with a positive, prudent and personalized education in the Catholic teaching on human sexuality?
- Been to my children a good example of how to live the Catholic Faith?
- Prayed with and for my children?
- Lived in humble obedience to those who legitimately exercise authority over me?
- Have I broken the law?
- Have I supported or voted for a politician whose positions are opposed to the teachings of Christ and the Catholic Church?

FIFTH COMMANDMENT

You shall not kill.

Have I...

- Unjustly and intentionally killed a human being?
- Been involved in an abortion, directly or indirectly (through advice, and so on)?
- Seriously considered or attempted suicide?
- Supported, promoted or encouraged the practice of assisted suicide or mercy killing?
- Deliberately desired to kill an innocent human being?
- Unjustly inflicted bodily harm another person?
- Unjustly threatened another person with bodily harm?
- Verbally or emotionally abused another person?
- Hated another person, or wished him evil?

- Been prejudiced, or unjustly discriminated against others because of their race, color, nationality, sex or religion?
- Joined a hate group?
- Purposely provoked another by teasing or nagging?
- Recklessly endangered my life or health, or that of another, by my actions?
- Driven recklessly or under the influence of alcohol or other drugs?
- Abused alcohol or other drugs?
- Sold or given drugs to others to use for non-therapeutic purposes?
- Used tobacco immoderately?
- Over-eaten?
- Encouraged others to sin by giving scandal?
- Helped another to commit a mortal sin (through advice, driving them somewhere, and so on)?
- Caused serious injury or death by criminal neglect?
- Indulged in serious anger?
- Refused to control my temper?
- Been mean to, quarreled with, or willfully hurt someone?
- Been unforgiving to others, when mercy or pardon was requested?
- Sought revenge or hoped something bad would happen to someone?
- Delighted to see someone else get hurt or suffer?
- Treated animals cruelly, causing them to suffer or die needlessly?

SIXTH AND NINTH COMMANDMENTS

You shall not commit adultery. You shall not covet your neighbor's wife.
Have I...

- Practiced the virtue of chastity?
- Given in to lust? (The desire for sexual pleasure unrelated to spousal love in marriage.)
- Used an artificial means of birth control?
- Refused to be open to conception, without just cause? (*Catechism*, 2368)
- Participated in immoral techniques for in vitro fertilization or artificial insemination?
- Sterilized my sex organs for contraceptive purposes?
- Deprived my spouse of the marital right, without just cause?
- Claimed my own marital right without concern for my spouse?
- Deliberately caused male climax outside of normal sexual intercourse? (*Catechism*, 2366)
- Willfully entertained impure thoughts?
- Purchased, viewed, or made use of pornography?
- Watched movies and television that involve sex and nudity?

- Listened to music or jokes that are harmful to purity?
- Committed adultery? (Sexual relations with someone who is married, or with someone other than my spouse.)
- Committed incest? (Sexual relations with a relative or in-law.)
- Committed fornication? (Sexual relations with someone of the opposite sex when neither of us is married.)
- Engaged in homosexual activity? (Sexual activity with someone of the same sex.)
- Committed rape?
- Masturbated? (Deliberate stimulation of one's own sexual organs for sexual pleasure.)
- Engaged in sexual foreplay (petting) reserved for marriage?
- Preyed upon children or youth for my sexual pleasure?
- Engaged in unnatural sexual activities?
- Engaged in prostitution, or paid for the services of a prostitute?
- Seduced someone, or allowed myself to be seduced?
- Made uninvited and unwelcome sexual advances toward another?
- Purposely dressed immodestly?

SEVENTH AND TENTH COMMANDMENTS

You shall not steal. You shall not covet your neighbor's goods.
Have I...

- Stolen? (Take something that doesn't belong to me against the reasonable will of the owner.)
- Envied others on account of their possessions?
- Tried to live in a spirit of Gospel poverty and simplicity?
- Given generously to others in need?
- Considered that God has provided me with money so that I might use it to benefit others, as well as for my own legitimate needs?
- Freed myself from a consumer mentality?
- Practiced the works of mercy?
- Deliberately defaced, destroyed or lost another's property?
- Cheated on a test, taxes, sports, games, or in business?
- Squandered money in compulsive gambling?
- Make a false claim to an insurance company?
- Paid my employees a living wage, or failed to give a full day's work for a full day's pay?
- Failed to honor my part of a contract?
- Failed to make good on a debt?
- Overcharge someone, especially to take advantage of another's hardship or ignorance?
- Misused natural resources?

EIGHTH COMMANDMENT

You shall not bear false witness against your neighbor.

Have I...

- Lied?
- Knowingly and willfully deceived another?
- Perjured myself under oath?
- Gossiped?
- Committed detraction? (Destroying a person's reputation by telling others about his faults for no good reason.)
- Committed slander or calumny? (Telling lies about another person in order to destroy his reputation.)
- Committed libel? (Writing lies about another person in order to destroy his reputation.)
- Been guilty of rash judgment? (Assuming the worst of another person based on circumstantial evidence.)
- Failed to make reparation for a lie I told, or for harm done to a person's reputation?
- Failed to speak out in defense of the Catholic Faith, the Church, or of another person?
- Betrayed another's confidence through speech?

The Precepts of the Church

FIRST PRECEPT

You shall attend Mass on Sundays and Holy Days of Obligation.

- (see examination under the Third Commandment)

SECOND PRECEPT

You shall confess your sins at least once a year.

Have I...

- Made a good Confession of my mortal sins least once a year?
- Purposely omitted telling my mortal sins in my last Confession?
- Performed the penance I was given?
- Made reparation for any harm I have done to others?

THIRD PRECEPT

You shall humbly receive your Creator in Holy Communion at least during the Easter season.

Have I...

- Fulfilled my Easter duty to receive Holy Communion at least once between the First Sunday of Lent and Trinity Sunday?

- Received Holy Communion while in the state of mortal sin?
- Fasted an hour before receiving Holy Communion?
- Received Holy Communion more than twice in one day?

FOURTH PRECEPT
You shall keep holy the Holy days of Obligation.
- (see examination under the Third Commandment)

FIFTH PRECEPT
You shall observe the prescribed days of fasting and abstinence.
Have I...

- Done penance every Friday, if not abstaining from meat, then some other form of penance?
- Abstained from meat on Ash Wednesday and the Fridays of Lent (if I am 14 years of age or older)?
- Fasted on Ash Wednesday and Good Friday (if I am between the ages of 18 and 59)?
- Spent time in prayer, doing spiritual and corporal works of mercy, and practicing self-denial?

SIXTH PRECEPT
You shall contribute to the support of the Church.
Have I...

- Contributed a just amount of my time, talents and money to support my parish and the work of the Church?

SEVENTH PRECEPT
You shall observe the laws of the Church concerning marriage.
Have I...

- Been living in a valid and licit marriage according to the laws of the Catholic Church?
- Abandoned my spouse and family by separation or divorce?
- Kept company with someone whom I cannot marry in the Catholic Church?
- Given scandal by living with a member of the opposite sex without the benefit of a marriage blessed by the Catholic Church?
- Entered into marriage with more than one person at the same time?

The Seven Deadly Sins

While the above examination of conscience is fairly exhaustive, some find it helpful to use the Seven Deadly Sins in examining their consciences. Revs. John Trigilio, Jr. and Kenneth Brighenti have provided a list of these sins along with a fairly detailed explanation of each of them, along with the opposing virtues. This list should prove helpful in preparing one for the Sacrament of Reconciliation.
(http://www.dummies.com/how-to/content/the-seven-deadly-sins-of-the-catholic-church.html)

"The seven deadly sins are:

1. **Pride:** The inordinate love of self — a super-confidence and high esteem in your own abilities also known as *vanity*. Pride fools you into thinking that you're the source of your own greatness. Liking yourself isn't sinful. In fact, it's healthy and necessary, but when the self-perception no longer conforms to reality, and you begin to think that you're more important than you actually are, the sin of pride is rearing its ugly head.

   Pride is the key to all other sins, because after you believe that you're more important than you actually are, you compensate for it when others don't agree with your judgment. You rationalize your behavior and make excuses for lying, cheating, stealing, insulting, ignoring, and such, because no one understands you like *you* do. In your mind, you're underestimated by the world. Humility is the best remedy for pride. Catholicism regards humility as recognizing that talent is really a gift from God.

2. **Envy:** Resenting another person's good fortune or joy. Catholicism distinguishes between two kinds of envy: **Material envy** is when you resent others who have more money, talent, strength, beauty, friends, and so on, than you do. **Spiritual envy** is resenting others who progress in holiness, preferring that they stay at or below your level instead of being joyful and happy that they're doing what they're supposed to be doing. Spiritual envy is far worse and more evil than material envy. The Church maintains that meekness or kindness can counter envy.

3. **Lust:** Looking at, imagining, and treating others as mere sex objects to serve your own physical pleasures, rather than as individuals made in the image and likeness of God. The Catholic Church believes that

it's normal and healthy to be attracted to and to appreciate the opposite sex. That's not lust and it's not considered a sin. Chastity, the virtue that moderates sexual desire, is the best remedy for lust. Chastity falls under temperance and can help to keep physical pleasure in moderation.

4. **Anger:** The sudden outburst of emotion — namely hostility — and thoughts about the desire for revenge. You have no control over what angers you, but you do have control over what you do after you become angry. Even if someone does you wrong — robs you, for example — to avoid the sin of anger, you don't go after the thief yourself, you desire for the police to catch the thief and for a court to sentence her to a fair punishment. Patience, the virtue that allows you to adapt and endure evil without harboring any destructive feelings, is the best countermeasure for anger.

5. **Gluttony:** Choosing to over-consume food or alcohol. Enjoying a delightful dinner isn't sinful, but intentionally overeating to the point where you literally get sick to your stomach is. So, too, having an alcoholic beverage now and then (provided that you don't suffer from alcoholism) is *not* sinful in the eyes of the Church. But drinking to the point of drunkenness is. Legitimate eating disorders, such as anorexia and bulimia, aren't gluttony. They're medical conditions that require treatment and care. Gluttony is voluntary and merely requires self-control and moderation. Periodic *fasting,* restricting the amount of food you eat, and *abstinence,* avoiding meat or some favorite food, are the best defenses against gluttony.

6. **Greed:** The inordinate love of and desire for earthly possessions. Amassing a fortune and trying to accumulate the most stuff is greed, sometimes called *avarice.* Next to anger, envy, and lust, more crimes have been committed due to greed than any other deadly sin. Generosity is the best weapon against greed. Freely giving some of your possessions away, especially to those less fortunate, is considered the perfect antithesis to greed and avarice.

7. **Sloth:** (sometimes called *acedia*) is laziness — particularly when it concerns prayer and spiritual life. Sloth is always wanting to rest and relax, with no desire or intention of making a sacrifice or doing something for others. It's an aversion to work — physical, mental, and spiritual. The Church says that the evil habit of being inattentive at religious worship services and being careless in fulfilling your religious duties is also a sin of sloth." (Source:

119

http://www.dummies.com/how-to/content/the-seven-deadly-sins-of-the-catholic-church.html).

Acts of Contrition

There are many different acts of contrition that can be used in the confessional, ranging from the very simple ejaculation, "Lord, Jesus Christ, have mercy on me, a sinner," all the way to Psalm 51, a most beautiful penitential psalm. Speaking on penance and contrition, the Catechism of the Catholic Church states, "Jesus' call to conversion and penance, like that of the prophets before Him, does not aim first at outward works, "sackcloth and ashes," fasting and mortification, but at the conversion of the heart, interior conversion." Without this, such penances remain sterile and false; however, interior conversion urges expression in visible signs, gestures and works of penance.

"Interior repentance is a radical reorientation of our whole life, a return, a conversion to God with all our heart, an end of sin, a turning away from evil, with repugnance toward the evil actions we have committed. At the same time it entails the desire and resolution to change one's life, with hope in God's mercy and trust in the help of His grace" (CCC, 1430-31). Traditional acts of contrition that can be recited at the end of your confession to the priest, are printed below for your convenience:

TRADITIONAL ACT OF CONTRITION

O my God, I am heartily sorry for having offended Thee, and I detest all my sins, because I dread the loss of heaven, and the pains of hell; but most of all because they offend Thee, my God, Who are all good and deserving of all my love. I firmly resolve, with the help of Thy grace, to confess my sins, to do penance, and to amend my life. Amen.

Penitential Psalm 51 – Miserere

"Have mercy on me, O God, according to thy great mercy. And according to the multitude of thy tender mercies blot out my iniquity. Wash me yet more from my iniquity, and cleanse me from my sin. For I know my iniquity, and my sin is always before me. To thee only have I sinned, and have done evil before thee: that thou mayest be justified in thy words and mayst overcome when thou art judged. For behold I was conceived in iniquities; and in sins did my mother conceive me. For behold thou hast loved truth: the uncertain and hidden things of thy wisdom thou hast made manifest to me. Thou shalt sprinkle me with hyssop, and I shall be cleansed: thou shalt wash me, and I shall be made whiter than snow. To my hearing thou shalt give joy and gladness: and the bones that have been humbled shall rejoice."

"Turn away thy face from my sins, and blot out all my iniquities. Create a clean heart in me, O God: and renew a right spirit within my bowels. Cast me not away from thy face; and take not thy holy spirit from me. Restore unto me the joy of thy salvation, and strengthen me with a perfect spirit. I will teach the unjust thy ways: and the wicked shall be converted to thee. Deliver me from blood, O God, thou God of my salvation: and my tongue shall extol thy justice. O Lord, thou wilt open my lips: and my mouth shall declare thy praise. For if thou hadst desired sacrifice, I would indeed have given it: with burnt offerings thou wilt not be delighted. A sacrifice to God is an afflicted spirit: a contrite and humbled heart, O God, thou wilt not despise. Deal favourably, O Lord, in thy good will with Sion; that the walls of Jerusalem may be built up. Then shalt thou accept the sacrifice of justice, oblations and whole burnt offerings: then shall they lay calves upon thy altar."

14.   THE DAILY ROSARY

The Prayer Most Pleasing to Our Lady

After the Holy Sacrifice of the Mass and the Liturgy of the Hours, the Rosary of our Blessed Lady is widely considered the "highest" or "best" form of Catholic prayer, and this due to the fact that we meditate on the mysteries of Christ's life, death and resurrection through, with and in Mary, Queen of Contemplation. In each well-prayed Rosary, the Mother truly unites her most beautiful and powerful voice to ours, so that our prayer will become pleasing to the Most Holy Trinity.

The Rosary involves both meditative and vocal prayer. That is, as we meditate on any of the 20 mysteries of the Rosary, we simultaneously pray out loud to Our Lady, rendering her the praise and veneration that is her due, and asking her to exercise her maternal mediation on our behalf. Countless saints, mystics and popes have hailed the Rosary of our Blessed Mother as one of the single most salutary and efficacious of devotions, and the Mother of God herself has come from heaven to reveal the treasures of grace hidden in the Rosary. The rosary can alter world events: it can stop wars, put an end to the holocaust of abortion, and hasten the promised Triumph of the Immaculate Heart in the world. Moreover, while more and more individuals and families adopt the daily recitation of the Rosary, there will come about the peace of Christ in the heart of the individual, which, in turn, will lead to peace in families, and ultimately, to peace amongst nations and throughout the world.

What is more, it should be noted that the praying of the Rosary is simultaneously the renewal and the expression of our total consecration to the Virgin Mary. Later in this chapter, we shall list the fifteen promises given by Our Lady to Blessed Alan de la Roche. For now, let us suffice with a list of some of the truly amazing statements that have been made by Our Lady herself, various popes and saints on the utter efficacy of the prayer of the Rosary:

"Continue to pray the Rosary every day." (**Our Lady of Fatima to Sister Lucia**).

"Never will anyone who says his Rosary every day be led astray. This is a statement that I would gladly sign with my blood" (**Saint Louis de Montfort**).

"You shall obtain all you ask of me by the recitation of the Rosary" (**Our Lady to Blessed Alan de la Roche**).

"Give me an army saying the Rosary and I will conquer the world" (**Pope Blessed Pius IX**).

"If you persevere in reciting the Rosary, this will be a most probable sign of your eternal salvation" (**Blessed Alan de la Roche**).

"The greatest method of praying is to pray the Rosary" (**Saint Francis de Sales**).

"When the Holy Rosary is said well, it gives Jesus and Mary more glory and is more meritorious than any other prayer" (**Saint Louis de Montfort**).

"The Holy Rosary is the storehouse of countless blessing" (**Blessed Alan de la Roche**).

"One day, through the Rosary and the Scapular, Our Lady will save the world" (**Saint Dominic**).

"If you say the Rosary faithfully unto death, I do assure you that, in spite of the gravity of your sins, 'you will receive a never-fading crown of glory' (1 St. Peter 5:4)" (**Saint Louis de Montfort**).

"The Rosary is THE weapon" (**Saint Pio of Pietrelcina** [Padre Pio]).

"You must know that when you 'hail' Mary, she immediately greets you! Don't think that she is one of those rude women of whom there are so many—on the contrary, she is utterly courteous and pleasant. If you greet her, she will answer you right away and converse with you!" (**Saint Bernardine of Siena**).

"Recite your Rosary with faith, with humility, with confidence, and with perseverance" (**Saint Louis de Montfort**).

"The Rosary is the most beautiful and the most rich in graces of all prayers; it is the prayer that touches most the Heart of the Mother of God...and if you wish peace to reign in your homes, recite the family Rosary" (**Pope Saint Pius X**).

"Never will anyone who says his Rosary every day, become a formal heretic or be led astray by the devil" **(Saint Louis de Montfort)**.

"Even if you are on the brink of damnation, even if you have one foot in hell, even if you have sold your soul to the devil as sorcerers do who practice black magic, and even if you are a heretic as obstinate as a devil, sooner or later you will be converted and will amend your life and will save your soul, if—and mark well what I say—if you say the Holy Rosary devoutly every day until death for the purpose of knowing the truth and obtaining contrition and pardon for your sins" **(Saint Louis de Montfort)**.

"The Most Holy Virgin in these last times in which we live has given a new efficacy to the recitation of the Rosary to such an extent that there is no problem, no matter how difficult it is, whether temporal or above all spiritual, in the personal life of each one of us, of our families…that cannot be solved by the Rosary. There is no problem, I tell you, no matter how difficult it is, that we cannot resolve by the prayer of the Holy Rosary" **(Sister Lucia dos Santos, Fatima seer)**.

"When you say your Rosary, the angels rejoice, the Blessed Trinity delights in it, my Son finds joy in it too, and I myself am happier than you can possibly guess. After the Holy Sacrifice of the Mass, there is nothing in the Church that I love as much as the Rosary" **(Our Lady to Blessed Alan de la Roche)**.

"'Hail Mary, full of grace, the Lord is with thee!' No creature has ever said anything that was more pleasing to me, nor will anyone ever be able to find or say to me anything that pleases me more" **(Our Lady to Saint Mechtilde)**.

(Source: http://catholiccampuswatch.blogspot.com/2010/11/quotes-of-our-lady-popes-and-saints.html)

The traditional Dominican Rosary of Our Lady is composed of five sets of ten small beads, separated by 5 large beads. Each bead on the small set of 10 represents one "Hail Mary." The "Our Father" is prayed on the large beads. Meditation on the Mysteries of the Holy Rosary constitutes the "heart" of this devotion. Traditionally, there were three sets of Mysteries; the Joyful, the Sorrowful and the Glorious. Pope John Paul II recently made a marvelous contribution to the history of the Rosary by adding a fourth set of mysteries, the Mysteries of Light, or the Luminous Mysteries.

The five Joyful Mysteries, prayed on Monday and Saturday:

1. The Annunciation, 2. The Visitation, 3. The Nativity, 4. The Presentation of Our Lord in the Temple, 5. The Finding of Jesus in the Temple.

The five Sorrowful Mysteries, prayed on Tuesday and Friday:

1. The Agony in the Garden; 2. The Scourging at the Pillar, 3. The Crowning with Thorns, 4. The Carrying of the Cross, 5. The Crucifixion.

The five Glorious Mysteries, prayed on Wednesday and Sunday:

1. The Resurrection, 2. The Ascension, 3. The Decent of the Holy Spirit at Pentecost, 4. The Assumption of Mary, Body and Soul, into Heaven, 5. The Coronation of Mary as Queen of Heaven and Earth.

The five Luminous Mysteries, prayed on Thursday:

1. The Baptism of Jesus, 2. The Wedding at Cana, 3. Proclaiming the Kingdom of God, 4. The Transfiguration, 5. The Eucharist.

How to Pray the Rosary

1. While holding the Crucifix in your hand, recite the: "Apostles Creed" I believe in God the Father Almighty, Creator of Heaven and earth; and in Jesus Christ, His only Son, our Lord, Who was conceived by the Holy Ghost, born of the Virgin Mary, suffered under Pontius Pilate, was crucified, died and was buried; He descended into hell; the third day He arose again from the dead; He ascended into Heaven, and sitteth at the right hand of God, the Father Almighty; From thence He shall come to judge the living and the dead. I believe in the Holy Ghost, the Holy Catholic Church, the Communion of Saints, the forgiveness of sins, the resurrection of the body, and life everlasting. Amen."

2. On the first bead recite the: "Our Father:" "Our Father Who art in Heaven, hallowed be Thy Name; Thy kingdom come; Thy will be done on earth as it is in Heaven. Give us this day our daily bread, and forgive us our trespasses, as we forgive those who trespass against us, and lead us not into temptation, but deliver us from evil. Amen."

3. On the three small beads recite the "Hail Mary" for an increase in the supernatural virtues of Faith, Hope and Charity. "Hail Mary, full of grace, the Lord is with thee; blessed art thou among women, and

blessed is the fruit of thy womb, Jesus. Holy Mary, Mother of God, pray for us sinners, now and at the hour of our death. Amen."

4. Recite the "Glory Be:" "Glory be to the Father, and to the Son, and to the Holy Ghost, as it was in the beginning, is now, and ever shall be, world without end. Amen."

5. Calls to mind the Mystery and reflect upon it then on the large bead recite, the "Our Father."

6. On the ten small beads, recite the "Hail Mary" keeping in mind the mystery.

7. Recite the "Glory Be."

8. Repeat steps 5-7 until you have completed the five decades of the Rosary.

9. Conclude the Rosary by praying the Salve Regina: "Hail, Holy Queen, Mother of Mercy, our life, our sweetness, and our hope; to Thee do we come, poor banished children of Eve; to Thee do we send up our sighs, mourning and weeping in this vale of tears. Turn, then, most gracious Advocate, Thine eyes of mercy toward us, and after this, our exile, show unto us the most blessed fruit of Thy womb, Jesus, O clement, O loving, O sweet Virgin Mary."

The Scriptural Rosary

What follows is a more meditative, reflective, and contemplative way to pray the Rosary. It is called the Scriptural Rosary due to the fact that one is provided with a passage from Sacred Scripture for each of the "Hail Mary" prayers. Thus, one truly enters into the mystery being meditated upon using Sacred Scripture as a guide. The Scriptural Rosary was a popular way to pray the rosary in the middle ages. Gratefully, this method has made a major comeback with the publication of "The Scriptural Rosary," a handbook that provides quotations from Scripture for each "Hail Mary" prayer. Below, you will find a version of the Scriptural Rosary that you can use in your own prayer of the Rosary. I pray that this devotional deepens your experience of the mysteries of the Holy Rosary.

THE FIRST JOYFUL MYSTERY – The Annunciation

Our Father…

1. In the sixth month the angel Gabriel was sent from God to a city of Galilee named Nazareth, to a virgin betrothed to a man whose name was Joseph; of the house of David; and the virgin's name was Mary (Lk 1:26-27) Hail Mary
2. And [Gabriel] came to her and said, "Hail, full of grace, the Lord is with you!" (Lk 1:28) Hail Mary
3. But she was greatly troubled at the saying and considered in her mind what sort of greeting this might be (Lk 1:29) Hail Mary
4. And the angel said to her, "Do not be afraid, Mary, for you have found favor with God" (Lk 1:30) Hail Mary
5. "And behold, you will conceive in your womb and bear a son, and you shall call his name Jesus" (Lk 1:31) Hail Mary
6. "He will be great and will be called Son of the Most High; and the Lord God will give to him the throne of his father David, and he will reign over the house of Jacob forever; and of his kingdom there will be no end" (Lk 1:32-33) Hail Mary
7. And Mary said to the angel, "How can this be, since I have no husband?" (Lk 1:34) Hail Mary
8. And the angel said to her, "The Holy Spirit will come upon you and the power of the Most High will overshadow you" (Lk 1:35) Hail Mary
9. "Therefore the child to be born will be called holy, the Son of God" (Lk 1:35) Hail Mary
10. And Mary said, "Behold, I am the handmaid of the Lord; let it be to me according to your word" (Lk 1:38) Hail Mary

Glory be to the Father, and to the Son, and to the Holy Spirit. As it was in the beginning, is now, and ever shall be, world without end. Amen.

Fatima Prayer: Oh my Jesus, forgive us our sins. Save us from the fires of hell. Lead all souls to Heaven, especially those in most need of Thy mercy.

THE SECOND JOYFUL MYSTERY – The Visitation

Our Father…

1. In those days Mary arose and went with haste into the hill country, to a city of Judah, and she entered the house of Zechariah and greeted Elizabeth (Lk 1:39-40) Hail Mary

2. And when Elizabeth heard the greeting of Mary, the child leaped in her womb; and Elizabeth was filled with the Holy Spirit (Lk 1:41) Hail Mary

3. And she exclaimed with a loud cry, "Blessed are you among women, and blessed is the fruit of your womb!" (Lk 1:42) Hail Mary

4. "And blessed is she who believed that there would be a fulfillment of what was spoken to her from the Lord" (Lk 1:45) Hail Mary

5. And Mary said, "My soul magnifies the Lord, and my spirit rejoices in God my Savior, for he has regarded the low estate of his handmaiden" (Lk 1:46-48) Hail Mary

6. "For behold, henceforth all generations will call me blessed; for he who is mighty has done great things for me" (Lk 1:48-49) Hail Mary

7. "And holy is his name. And his mercy is on those who fear him from generation to generation" (Lk 1:49-50) Hail Mary

8. "He has shown strength with his arm, he has scattered the proud in the imagination of their hearts" (Lk 1:51) Hail Mary

9. "He has put down the mighty from their thrones, and exalted those of low degree" (Lk 1:52) Hail Mary

10. "He has filled the hungry with good things, and the rich he has sent empty away" (Lk 1:53) Hail Mary

Glory be to the Father, and to the Son, and to the Holy Spirit. As it was in the beginning, is now, and ever shall be, world without end. Amen.

Fatima Prayer: Oh my Jesus, forgive us our sins. Save us from the fires of hell. Lead all souls to Heaven, especially those in most need of Thy mercy.

THE THIRD JOYFUL MYSTERY – The Nativity
Our Father…

1. And while Mary and Joseph were in Bethlehem, the time came for her to be delivered (Lk 2:6) Hail Mary

2. And she gave birth to her firstborn son and wrapped him in swaddling clothes (Lk 2:7) Hail Mary

3. And she laid him in a manger, because there was no place for them in the inn (Lk 2:7) Hail Mary

4. And in that region there were shepherds out in the field, keeping watch over their flock by night. And an angel of the Lord appeared to them, and the glory of the Lord shone around them, and they were filled with fear (Lk 2:8-9) Hail Mary

5. And the angel said to them, "Be not afraid; for behold, I bring you news of a great joy which will come to all the people" (Lk 2:10) Hail Mary

6. "For to you is born this day in the city of David a Savior, who is Christ the Lord" (Lk 2:11) Hail Mary
7. "Glory to God in the highest, and on earth peace among men with whom he is pleased!" (Lk 2:14) Hail Mary
8. And going into the house, the Wise Men saw the child with Mary his mother (Mt 2:1, 11) Hail Mary
9. And they fell down and worshipped him. Then, opening their treasures, they offered him gifts, gold and frankincense and myrrh (Mt 2:11) Hail Mary
10. But Mary kept all these things pondering them in her heart. (Lk 2:19) Hail Mary

Glory be to the Father, and to the Son, and to the Holy Spirit. As it was in the beginning, is now, and ever shall be, world without end. Amen.

Fatima Prayer: Oh my Jesus, forgive us our sins. Save us from the fires of hell. Lead all souls to Heaven, especially those in most need of Thy mercy.

THE FOURTH JOYFUL MYSTERY – The Presentation
Our Father…

1. And when the time came for their purification according to the law of Moses, Mary and Joseph took Jesus up to Jerusalem to present him to the Lord (Lk 2:22) Hail Mary
2. Now there was a man in Jerusalem whose name was Simeon and this man was righteous and devout, looking for the consolation of Israel, and the Holy Spirit was upon him (Lk 2:25) Hail Mary
3. And it had been revealed to him by the Holy Spirit that he should not see death before he had seen the Lord's Christ (Lk 2:26) Hail Mary
4. And inspired by the Spirit, Simeon came into the temple; and when the parents brought in the child Jesus, to do for him according to the custom of the law, he took him up in his arms and blessed God (Lk 2:27-28) Hail Mary
5. "Lord, now let your servant depart in peace, according to your word" (Lk 2:29) Hail Mary
6. "For my eyes have seen your salvation which you have prepared in the presence of all peoples" (Lk 2:30-31) Hail Mary
7. "A light for revelation to the Gentiles and for glory to your people Israel" (Lk 2:32) Hail Mary
8. And Simeon blessed them and said to Mary his mother, "Behold, this child is set for the fall and the rising of many in Israel, and for a sign that is spoken against" (Lk 2:34) Hail Mary

9. "And a sword will pierce through your own soul also, that thoughts out of many hearts may be revealed" (Lk 2:35) Hail Mary
10. And when they performed everything according to the law of the Lord, they returned into Galilee, to their own city, Nazareth. And the child grew and became strong, filled with wisdom; and the favor of God was upon him (Lk 2:39-40) Hail Mary

Glory be to the Father, and to the Son, and to the Holy Spirit. As it was in the beginning, is now, and ever shall be, world without end. Amen.

Fatima Prayer: Oh my Jesus, forgive us our sins. Save us from the fires of hell. Lead all souls to Heaven, especially those in most need of Thy mercy.

THE FIFTH JOYFUL MYSTERY – The Finding of Jesus in the Temple
Our Father…

1. Now Jesus's parents went to Jerusalem every year at the feast of the Passover. And when Jesus was twelve years old, they went up according to custom (Lk 2:41-42) Hail Mary
2. And when the feast was ended, as they were returning, the boy Jesus stayed behind in Jerusalem. His parents did not know it (Lk 2:43) Hail Mary
3. And when they did not find him, they returned to Jerusalem seeking him. After three days, they found him in the temple (Lk 2:45-46) Hail Mary
4. He was sitting among the teachers, listening to them, and asking them questions (Lk 2:46) Hail Mary
5. And all who heard him were amazed at his understanding and his answers (Lk 2:47) Hail Mary
6. And his mother said to him, "Son, why have you treated us so? Behold, your father and I have been looking for you anxiously" (Lk 2:48) Hail Mary
7. And he said to them, "How is it that you sought me? Did you not know that I must be in my Father's house?" (Lk 2:49) Hail Mary
8. And they did not understand the saying which he spoke to them (Lk 2:50) Hail Mary
9. And he went down with them and came to Nazareth, and was obedient to them (Lk 2:51) Hail Mary
10. And Jesus increased in wisdom and in stature, and in favor with God and man (Lk 2:52) Hail Mary

Glory be to the Father, and to the Son, and to the Holy Spirit. As it was in the beginning, is now, and ever shall be, world without end. Amen.

Fatima Prayer: Oh my Jesus, forgive us our sins. Save us from the fires of hell. Lead all souls to Heaven, especially those in most need of Thy mercy.

THE FIRST SORROWFUL MYSTERY – The Agony in the Garden
Our Father...

1. Then Jesus went with them to a place called Gethsemane. And he began to be sorrowful and troubled (Mt 26:36-37) Hail Mary
2. Then he said to them, "My soul is very sorrowful, even to death; remain here, and watch with me" (Mt 26:38) Hail Mary
3. And he withdrew from them about a stone's throw, and knelt down and prayed (Lk 22:41) Hail Mary
4. "Father, if you are willing, remove this chalice from me; nevertheless not my will, but yours, be done" (Lk 22:42) Hail Mary
5. And there appeared to him an angel from heaven, strengthening him (Lk 22:43) Hail Mary
6. And being in agony he prayed more earnestly (Lk 22:44) Hail Mary
7. And his sweat became like great drops of blood falling down upon the ground (Lk 22:44) Hail Mary
8. And he came back to his disciples and found them sleeping; and he said to Peter, "So, could you not watch with me one hour?" (Mt 26:40) Hail Mary
9. "Watch and pray that you may not enter into temptation" (Mt 26:41) Hail Mary
10. "The spirit indeed is willing, but the flesh is weak" (Mt 26:41) Hail Mary

Glory be to the Father, and to the Son, and to the Holy Spirit. As it was in the beginning, is now, and ever shall be, world without end. Amen.

Fatima Prayer: Oh my Jesus, forgive us our sins. Save us from the fires of hell. Lead all souls to Heaven, especially those in most need of Thy mercy.

THE SECOND SORROWFUL MYSTERY – The Scourging at the Pillar
Our Father...

1. And as soon as it was morning the chief priests, with the elders and scribes, and the whole council held a consultation; and they bound

Jesus and led him away and delivered him to Pilate. And Pilate asked him, "Are you the king of the Jews?" (Mk 15:1-2) Hail Mary

2. Jesus answered, "My kingdom is not of this world; if my kingship were of this world, my servants would fight, that I might not be handed over to the Jews; but my kingship is not from the world" (Jn 18:36) Hail Mary

3. Pilate said to him, "So you are a king?" Jesus answered, "You say that I am a king. For this I was born, and for this I have come into the world, to bear witness to the truth. Everyone who is of the truth hears my voice" (Jn 18:37) Hail Mary

4. Pilate said to him, "What is truth?" After he had said this, he went out to the Jews again and told them, "I find no crime in him" (Jn 18:38) Hail Mary

5. "I will therefore chastise him and release him." Then Pilate took Jesus and scourged him. (Lk 23:16, Jn 19:1) Hail Mary

6. He was despised and rejected by men; a man of sorrows, and acquainted with grief; and as one from whom men hide their faces he was despised, and we esteemed him not (Is 53:3) Hail Mary

7. He was oppressed, and he was afflicted, yet he opened not his mouth; like a lamb that is led to the slaughter, and like a sheep that before its shearers is silent, so he opened not his mouth (Is 53:7) Hail Mary

8. But he was wounded for our transgressions, he was bruised for our iniquities (Is 53:5) Hail Mary

9. Surely he has borne our grief and carried our sorrows. Yet we esteemed him stricken, struck down by God, and afflicted (Is 53:4) Hail Mary

10. Upon him was the chastisement that made us whole, and with his stripes we are healed. (Is 53:5) Hail Mary

Glory be to the Father, and to the Son, and to the Holy Spirit. As it was in the beginning, is now, and ever shall be, world without end. Amen.

Fatima Prayer: Oh my Jesus, forgive us our sins. Save us from the fires of hell. Lead all souls to Heaven, especially those in most need of Thy mercy.

THE THIRD SORROWFUL MYSTERY – The Crowning with Thorns
Our Father...

1. And the soldiers led him away to the Praetorium. And they stripped him and put a scarlet robe upon him (Mk 15:16-17, Mt 27:28) Hail Mary

2. And plaiting a crown of thorns they put it on his head, and put a reed in his right hand (Mt 27:29) Hail Mary
3. And kneeling before him they mocked him, saying "Hail, king of the Jews!" (Mt 27:29) Hail Mary
4. And they spat upon him and took the reed and struck him on the head (Mt 27:30) Hail Mary
5. Then Pilate took water and washed his hands before the crowd, saying, "I am innocent of this righteous man's blood; see to it yourselves" (Mt 27:24) Hail Mary
6. So Jesus came out, wearing the crown of thorns and the purple robe (Jn 19:5) Hail Mary
7. Pilate said to the Jews, "Here is your King!" They cried out, "Away with him, away with him, crucify him!" (Jn 19:15) Hail Mary
8. And Pilate said to them, "Why, what evil has he done?" But they shouted all the more, "Crucify him" (Mk15:14) Hail Mary
9. "Shall I crucify your king?" The chief priests answered, "We have no king but Caesar" (Jn 19:15) Hail Mary
10. So Pilate, wishing to satisfy the crowd, released for them Barabbas; and having scourged Jesus, he delivered him to be crucified (Mk 15:15) Hail Mary

Glory be to the Father, and to the Son, and to the Holy Spirit. As it was in the beginning, is now, and ever shall be, world without end. Amen.

Fatima Prayer: Oh my Jesus, forgive us our sins. Save us from the fires of hell. Lead all souls to Heaven, especially those in most need of Thy mercy.

THE FOURTH SORROWFUL MYSTERY – The Carrying of the Cross
Our Father...

1. "If any man would come after me, let him deny himself" (Lk 9:23) Hail Mary
2. "And take up his cross daily and follow me" (Lk 9:23) Hail Mary
3. So they took Jesus, and he went out, carrying his own cross (Jn 19:17) Hail Mary
4. And as the led him away, they seized one Simon of Cyrene, who was coming in from the country, and laid on him the cross, to carry it behind Jesus (Lk 23:26) Hail Mary
5. "Take my yoke upon you and learn from me" (Mt 11:29) Hail Mary
6. "For I am gentle and lowly in heart." (Mt 11:29) Hail Mary
7. "And you will find rest for your souls. For my yoke is easy and my burden light" (Mt 11:29-30) Hail Mary

8. And there followed him a great multitude of the people, and of women who bewailed and lamented him (Lk 23:27) Hail Mary

9. But Jesus turning to them said, "Daughters of Jerusalem, do not weep for me, but weep for yourselves and for your children" (Lk 23:28) Hail Mary

10. "For if they do this when the wood is green, what will happen when it is dry?" (Lk 23:31) Hail Mary

Glory be to the Father, and to the Son, and to the Holy Spirit. As it was in the beginning, is now, and ever shall be, world without end. Amen.

Fatima Prayer: Oh my Jesus, forgive us our sins. Save us from the fires of hell. Lead all souls to Heaven, especially those in most need of Thy mercy.

THE FIFTH SORROWFUL MYSTERY – The Crucifixion of Our Lord Jesus Christ
Our Father...

1. And when they came to the place which is called The Skull, there they crucified him (Lk 23:33) Hail Mary

2. And Jesus said, "Father, forgive them; for they know not what they do" (Lk 23:34) Hail Mary

3. One of the criminals who were crucified with him said, "Jesus, remember me when you come in your kingly power" (Lk 23:39, 42; Mk 15:32) Hail Mary

4. "Truly, I say to you, today you will be with me in paradise" (Lk 23:43) Hail Mary

5. But standing by the cross of Jesus were his mother and the disciple whom he loved (Jn 19:25-26) Hail Mary

6. Jesus said to his mother, "Woman, behold, your son." Then he said to the disciple, "Behold, your mother" (Jn 19:26-27) Hail Mary

7. And from that hour the disciple took her to his own home (Jn 19:27) Hail Mary

8. And there was darkness over the whole land. And behold, the curtain of the temple was torn in two from top to bottom, and the earth shook (Lk 23:44; Mt 27:51) Hail Mary

9. Then Jesus, crying with a loud voice, said "Father, into your hands I commit my spirit!" (Lk 23:46) Hail Mary

10. And he bowed his head and gave up his spirit (Jn 19:30) Hail Mary

Glory be to the Father, and to the Son, and to the Holy Spirit. As it was in the beginning, is now, and ever shall be, world without end. Amen.

Fatima Prayer: Oh my Jesus, forgive us our sins. Save us from the fires of hell. Lead all souls to Heaven, especially those in most need of Thy mercy.

THE FIRST GLORIOUS MYSTERY – The Resurrection
Our Father...

1. "Truly, Truly, I say to you, you will weep and lament, but the world will rejoice; you will be sorrowful, but your sorrow will turn into joy" (Jn 16:20) Hail Mary
2. "But I will see you again, and your hearts will rejoice, and no one will take your joy from you" (Jn 16:22) Hail Mary
3. At the early dawn, they went to the tomb, taking the spices which they had prepared (Lk 24:1) Hail Mary
4. For an angel of the Lord descended from heaven and came and rolled back the stone, and sat upon it (Mt 28:2) Hail Mary
5. "Do not be afraid; for I know that you seek Jesus who was crucified. He is not here" (Mt 28:5-6) Hail Mary
6. "For he has risen, as he said. Come, see the place where he lay" (Lk 24:6) Hail Mary
7. "He is going before you to Galilee; there you will see him" (Mt 28:7) Hail Mary
8. And the women went out and fled from the tomb with fear and great joy, and ran to tell his disciples (Mk 16:8; Mt 28:8) Hail Mary
9. "I am the resurrection and the life; he who believes in me, though he die, yet shall he live" (Jn 11:25) Hail Mary
10. "And whoever lives and believes in me shall never die" (Jn 11:26) Hail Mary

Glory be to the Father, and to the Son, and to the Holy Spirit. As it was in the beginning, is now, and ever shall be, world without end. Amen.

Fatima Prayer: Oh my Jesus, forgive us our sins. Save us from the fires of hell. Lead all souls to Heaven, especially those in most need of Thy mercy.

THE SECOND GLORIOUS MYSTERY – The Ascension
Our Father...

1. Then Jesus led them out as far as Bethany, and lifting up his hands he blessed them (Lk 24:50) Hail Mary
2. And Jesus came and said, "All authority in heaven and on earth has been given to me" (Mt 28:18) Hail Mary
3. "Go, therefore and make disciples of all nations" (Mt 28:19) Hail Mary

4. ". . . baptizing them in the name of the Father and of the Son and of the Holy Spirit" (Mt 28:19) Hail Mary
5. ". . . teaching them to observe all that I have commanded you" (Mt 28:20) Hail Mary
6. "He who believes and is baptized will be saved" (Mk 16:16) Hail Mary
7. "But he who does not believe will be condemned" (Mk 16:16) Hail Mary
8. "And behold, I am with you always, to the close of the age" (Mt 28:20) Hail Mary
9. And when he had said this, as they were looking on, he was lifted up, and a cloud took him out of their sight (Acts 1:9) Hail Mary
10. So then the Lord Jesus, after he had spoken to them, was taken up into heaven, and sat down at the right hand of God (Mk 16:19) Hail Mary

Glory be to the Father, and to the Son, and to the Holy Spirit. As it was in the beginning, is now, and ever shall be, world without end. Amen.

Fatima Prayer: Oh my Jesus, forgive us our sins. Save us from the fires of hell. Lead all souls to Heaven, especially those in most need of Thy mercy.

THE THIRD GLORIOUS MYSTERY – The Descent of the Holy Spirit
Our Father...

1. When the day of Pentecost day had come, they were all together in one place (Acts 2:1) Hail Mary
2. And suddenly a sound came from heaven like the rush of a mighty wind, and it filled all the house where they were sitting (Acts 2:2) Hail Mary
3. And there appeared to them tongues as of fire, distributed and resting on each one of them (Acts 2:3) Hail Mary
4. And they were all filled with the Holy Spirit, and began to tell the mighty works of God (Acts 2:4, 11) Hail Mary
5. Now there were dwelling in Jerusalem Jews, devout men from every nation under heaven (Acts 2:5) Hail Mary
6. But Peter, standing with the Eleven, lifted up his voice and addressed them (Acts 2:14) Hail Mary
7. And Peter said to them, "Repent, and be baptized every one of you in the name of Jesus Christ for the forgiveness of your sins; and you shall receive the gift of the Holy Spirit" (Acts 2:38) Hail Mary
8. So those who received his word were baptized, and there were added that day about three thousand souls (Acts 2:41) Hail Mary

9. Send forth your Spirit, and they shall be created; and you shall renew the face of the earth (Pentecost Alleluia) Hail Mary
10. Come, Holy Spirit, fill the hearts of your faithful; and enkindle in them the fire of your love (Pentecost Alleluia) Hail Mary

Glory be to the Father, and to the Son, and to the Holy Spirit. As it was in the beginning, is now, and ever shall be, world without end. Amen.

Fatima Prayer: Oh my Jesus, forgive us our sins. Save us from the fires of hell. Lead all souls to Heaven, especially those in most need of Thy mercy.

THE FOURTH GLORIOUS MYSTERY – The Assumption
Our Father...

1. "My beloved speaks and says to me: "Arise, my love, my dove, my fair one, and come away" (Songs 2:10) Hail Mary
2. "For behold, the winter is past, the rain is over and gone'" (Songs 2:11) Hail Mary
3. "Let me see your face, let me hear your voice, for your voice is sweet, and your face is comely" (Songs 2:14) Hail Mary
4. Then God's temple in heaven was opened, and the ark of his covenant was seen within his temple; and there were flashes of lightning, loud noises, peals of thunder, an earthquake, and heavy hail (Rev 11:19) Hail Mary
5. And a great sign appeared in heaven, a woman clothed with the sun (Rev 12:1) Hail Mary
6. . . . with the moon under her feet, and on her head a crown of twelve stars (Rev 12:1) Hail Mary
7. The daughter of the king is decked in her chamber with gold-woven robes; in many-colored robes she is led to the king (Psalm 45:13-14) Hail Mary
8. "O daughter, you are blessed by the Most High God above all women on earth" (Judith 13:18) Hail Mary
9. "Your hope will never depart from the hearts of men, as they remember the power of God" (Judith 13:19) Hail Mary
10. "You are the exaltation of Jerusalem, you are the great pride of our nation!" (Judith 15:9) Hail Mary

Glory be to the Father, and to the Son, and to the Holy Spirit. As it was in the beginning, is now, and ever shall be, world without end. Amen.

Fatima Prayer: Oh my Jesus, forgive us our sins. Save us from the fires of hell. Lead all souls to Heaven, especially those in most need of Thy mercy.

THE FIFTH GLORIOUS MYSTERY – The Coronation of the Virgin Mary as Queen of Heaven and earth

Our Father...

1. "Who is this that looks forth like the dawn, fair as the moon, bright as the sun?" (Songs 6:10) Hail Mary
2. "Like the rainbow gleaming in glorious clouds; like roses in the days of the first fruits" (Sir. 50:7-8) Hail Mary
3. "I am a rose of Sharon, a lily of the valleys" (Songs 2:1) Hail Mary
4. "My throne was in a pillar of cloud, and for eternity I shall not cease to exist" (Sir. 24:4,9) Hail Mary
5. "Come to me, you who desire me, and eat your fill of my produce" (Sir. 24:19) Hail Mary
6. "Like a terebinth I spread out my branches, my teaching is sweeter than honey" (Sir. 24:17,20) Hail Mary
7. "And now, my sons, listen to me; happy are those who keep my ways. Hear instruction and be wise" (Prov 8:32-33) Hail Mary
8. "Happy are those who keep my ways, watching daily at my gates' (Prov 8:32,34) Hail Mary
9. "For he who finds me finds life and obtains favor from the Lord" (Prov 8:35) Hail Mary
10. Hail, Queen of mercy, protect us from the enemy, and receive us at the hour of death (Queenship of the B.V.M., Gradual) Hail Mary

Glory be to the Father, and to the Son, and to the Holy Spirit. As it was in the beginning, is now, and ever shall be, world without end. Amen.

Fatima Prayer: Oh my Jesus, forgive us our sins. Save us from the fires of hell. Lead all souls to Heaven, especially those in most need of Thy mercy.

THE FIRST LUMINOUS MYSTERY – The Baptism in the Jordan

Our Father...

1. John the Baptist said, "I am the voice of one crying in the wilderness, 'Make straight the way of the Lord,' as the prophet Isaiah said" (Jn 1:23) Hail Mary
2. And John preached, saying, "After me comes he who is mightier than I, the thong of whose sandals I am not worthy to stoop down and untie" (Mk 1:7) Hail Mary
3. "I baptize you with water for repentance, but he who is coming after me will baptize you with the Holy Spirit and with fire" (Mt 3:11) Hail Mary

4. John saw Jesus coming toward him, and said, "Behold, the Lamb of God, who takes away the sin of the world!" (Jn 1:29) Hail Mary
5. Then Jesus came from Galilee to the Jordan to John, to be baptized by him (Mt 3:13) Hail Mary
6. John would have prevented him, saying, "I need to be baptized by you, and do you come to me?" (Mt 3:14) Hail Mary
7. But Jesus answered him, "Let it be so now, for thus it is fitting for us to fulfill all righteousness." Then John consented. (Mt 3:15) Hail Mary
8. And when Jesus was baptized, he went up immediately from the water, and behold, the heavens were opened, and he saw the Spirit of God descending like a dove / and alighting on him. (Mt 3:16) Hail Mary
9. And behold, a voice from heaven, saying, "This is my beloved Son, with whom I am well pleased" (Mt 3:17) Hail Mary
10. The Spirit immediately drove him out into the wilderness, and he was in the wilderness forty days, tempted by Satan. (Mk 1:12-13) Hail Mary

Glory be to the Father, and to the Son, and to the Holy Spirit. As it was in the beginning, is now, and ever shall be, world without end. Amen.

Fatima Prayer: Oh my Jesus, forgive us our sins. Save us from the fires of hell. Lead all souls to Heaven, especially those in most need of Thy mercy.

THE SECOND LUMINOUS MYSTERY – The Wedding at Cana
Our Father…

1. There was a marriage at Cana in Galilee, and the mother of Jesus was there (Jn 2:1) Hail Mary
2. When the wine failed, the mother of Jesus said to him, "They have no wine" (Jn 2:3) Hail Mary
3. And Jesus said to her, "O woman, what have you to do with me? My hour has not yet come" (Jn 2:4) Hail Mary
4. His mother said to the servers, "Do whatever he tells you" (Jn 2:5) Hail Mary
5. Now six stone jars were standing there, for the Jewish rites of purification, each holding twenty or thirty gallons (Jn 2:6) Hail Mary
6. Jesus said to them, "Fill the jars with water." And they filled them to the brim (Jn 2:7) Hail Mary
7. He said to them, "Now draw some out, and take it to the steward of the feast" (Jn 2:8) Hail Mary

8. When the steward of the feast tasted the water now become wine, and did not know where it came from, the steward of the feast called the bridegroom (Jn 2:9) Hail Mary

9. And the steward of the feast said to the bridegroom, "Every man serves the good wine first; and when men have drunk freely, then they bring out the poor wine; but you have kept the good wine until now" (Jn 2:10) Hail Mary

10. This, the first of his signs, Jesus did at Cana in Galilee, and manifested his glory, and his disciples believed in him (Jn 2:11) Hail Mary

Glory be to the Father, and to the Son, and to the Holy Spirit. As it was in the beginning, is now, and ever shall be, world without end. Amen.

Fatima Prayer: Oh my Jesus, forgive us our sins. Save us from the fires of hell. Lead all souls to Heaven, especially those in most need of Thy mercy.

THE THIRD LUMINOUS MYSTERY – The Proclamation of the Kingdom
Our Father...

1. Now after John was arrested, Jesus came into Galilee, preaching the gospel of God (Mk 1:14) Hail Mary

2. In him was life, and the life was the light of men. The light shines in the darkness, and the darkness has not overcome it (Jn 1:4-5) Hail Mary

3. Jesus said, "The time is fulfilled, and the kingdom of God is at hand; repent, and believe in the gospel" (Mk 1:15) Hail Mary

4. And many were gathered together, so that there was no longer room for them and he was preaching the word to them. (Mk 2:2) Hail Mary

5. And when they could not get near Jesus because of the crowd, they removed the roof above him; and when they had made an opening, they let down the pallet on which the paralytic lay (Mk 2:4) Hail Mary

6. "Which is easier, to say to the paralytic, 'Your sins are forgiven,' or to say, 'Rise, pick up your pallet and walk?'" (Mk 2:9) Hail Mary

7. "But that you may know that the Son of man has authority on earth to forgive sins" — he said to the paralytic — "I say to you, rise, take up your pallet and go home" (Mk 2:10-11) Hail Mary

8. And Jesus called to him his twelve disciples and gave them authority over unclean spirits, to cast them out, and to heal every disease and every infirmity (Mt 10:1) Hail Mary

9. These Twelve Jesus sent out charging them to preach, "The kingdom of heaven is at hand." (cf. Mt 10:5 & 7) Hail Mary

10. And when Jesus had said this, he breathed on them and said to them, "Receive the Holy Spirit. If you forgive the sins of any, they are forgiven; if you retain the sins of any, they are retained" (Jn 20:22-23) Hail Mary

Glory be to the Father, and to the Son, and to the Holy Spirit. As it was in the beginning, is now, and ever shall be, world without end. Amen.

Fatima Prayer: Oh my Jesus, forgive us our sins. Save us from the fires of hell. Lead all souls to Heaven, especially those in most need of Thy mercy.

THE FOURTH LUMINOUS MYSTERY – The Transfiguration of Our Lord
Our Father…

1. Now about eight days after these saying Jesus took with him Peter and John and James, and went up on the mountain to pray. (Lk 9:28) Hail Mary
2. And Jesus was transfigured before them, and his face shone like the sun, and his garments became white as light (Mt 17:2) Hail Mary
3. And behold, there appeared to them Moses and Elijah, talking with him (Mt 17:3) Hail Mary
4. Moses and Elijah spoke of Jesus's exodus that he was to accomplish in Jerusalem (Lk 9:31) Hail Mary
5. And Peter said to Jesus, "Lord, it is well that we are here; if you wish, I will make three booths here, one for you, one for Moses, and one for Elijah" (Mt 17:4) Hail Mary
6. As Peter said this, a cloud came and overshadowed them; and they were afraid as they entered the cloud. (Lk 9:34) Hail Mary
7. And a voice came out of the cloud, "This is my Son, my Chosen; listen to him!" (Lk 9:35) Hail Mary
8. And suddenly looking around they no longer saw any one with them but Jesus only (Mk 9:8) Hail Mary
9. And as they were coming down the mountain, Jesus charged them to tell no one what they had seen, until the Son of man should have risen from the dead (Mk 9:9) Hail Mary
10. So they kept the matter to themselves, questioning what the rising from the dead meant. (Mk 9:10) Hail Mary

Glory be to the Father, and to the Son, and to the Holy Spirit. As it was in the beginning, is now, and ever shall be, world without end. Amen.

Fatima Prayer: Oh my Jesus, forgive us our sins. Save us from the fires of hell. Lead all souls to Heaven, especially those in most need of Thy mercy.

THE FIFTH LUMINOUS MYSTERY – The Institution of the Eucharist

Our Father...

1. Now on the first day of Unleavened Bread, the disciples came to Jesus, saying, "Where will you have us prepare for you to eat the Passover?" (Mt 26:17) Hail Mary
2. Jesus said, "Go into the city to a such a one, and say to him, 'The Teacher says, My time is at hand; I will keep the Passover at your house with my disciples'" (Mt 26:18) Hail Mary
3. And when the hour came, he sat at table, and the apostles with him. And he said to them, "I have earnestly desired to eat this Passover with you before I suffer" (Lk 22:14-15) Hail Mary
4. And as they were eating, he said, "Truly, I say to you, one of you will betray me" (Mt 26:21) Hail Mary
5. Judas, who betrayed him, said, "Is it I, Master?" (Mt 26:25) Hail Mary
6. Now as they were eating, Jesus took bread, and blessed, and broke it, and gave it to the disciples and said, "Take, eat; this is my body" (Mt 26:26) Hail Mary
7. And he took a chalice, and when he had given thanks he gave it to them, saying, "Drink of it, all of you; for this is my blood of the covenant, which is poured out for many for the forgiveness of sins" (Mt 26:27-28) Hail Mary
8. For as often as you eat this bread and drink the chalice, you proclaim the Lord's death until he comes (1 Cor 11:26) Hail Mary
9. "I am the living bread which comes down from heaven; if any one eats of this bread, he will live forever; and the bread which I shall give for the life of the world is my flesh." (Jn 6:51) Hail Mary
10. "He who eats my flesh and drinks my blood has eternal life, and I will raise him at the last day" (Jn 6:54) Hail Mary

Glory be to the Father, and to the Son, and to the Holy Spirit. As it was in the beginning, is now, and ever shall be, world without end. Amen.

Fatima Prayer: Oh my Jesus, forgive us our sins. Save us from the fires of hell. Lead all souls to Heaven, especially those in most need of Thy mercy.

CONCLUDING PRAYER

Hail Holy Queen, Mother of Mercy, our life, our sweetness, and our hope. To thee do we cry, poor banished children of Eve. To thee do we send up

our sighs, mourning and weeping in this valley of tears. Turn then, most gracious advocate, thine eyes of mercy towards us, and after this, our exile, show unto us the blessed fruit of thy womb, Jesus. Oh Holy, Oh Clement, Oh Sweet Virgin Mary, pray for us, Oh Holy Mother of God, that we may be made worthy of the promises of Christ. Amen.
(Source: http://www.rosaryarmy.com/?page_id=586)

The Fifteen Promises of Mary for the Rosary

As given to St. Dominic and Blessed Alan:

1. Whoever shall faithfully serve me by the recitation of the rosary, shall receive signal graces.
2. I promise my special protection and the greatest graces to all those who shall recite the rosary.
3. The rosary will be a powerful armor against hell. It will destroy vice, decrease sin and defeat heresies.
4. It will cause virtue and good works to flourish; it will obtain for souls the abundant mercy of God; it will withdraw the hearts of men from the love of the world and its vanities, and will lift them to the desire of eternal things. Oh, that souls would sanctify themselves by this means.
5. Those who recommend themselves to me by the recitation of the Rosary shall not perish.
6. Whoever shall recite the rosary devoutly, applying himself to the consideration of its sacred mysteries shall never be conquered by misfortune. God will not chastise him in His justice, he shall not perish by an unprovided death; if he be just, he shall remain in the grace of God, and become worthy of eternal life.
7. Whoever shall have a true devotion for the rosary shall not die without the sacraments of the Church.
8. Those who are faithful to recite the rosary shall have during their life and at their death, the light of God and the plentitude of His graces; at the moment of death they shall participate in the merits of the saints in paradise.
9. I shall deliver from purgatory those who have been devoted to the rosary.
10. The faithful children of the rosary shall merit a high degree of glory in heaven.
11. You shall obtain all you ask of me by the recitation of the rosary.
12. All those who propagate the holy rosary shall be aided by me in their necessities.

13. I have obtained from my Divine Son that all the advocates of the rosary shall have for intercessors the entire celestial court during their life and at the hour of death.
14. All who recite the rosary are my sons, and brothers of my only son, Jesus Christ.
15. Devotion to my rosary is a great sign of predestination.

The following link will bring you to streaming audio of either the traditional rosary or the scriptural rosary:
http://www.rosaryarmy.com/?page_id=22

The link below enables one to pray the rosary in real time with others throughout the world: http://www.comepraytherosary.org/

A Plenary Indulgence may be gained (under the usual conditions) when the Rosary is prayed in Church, in a family group or in a religious community. Also:

- Five (5) decades of the Rosary must be prayed continuously.
- The prayers of the Rosary must be prayed vocally and one must meditate upon the Mysteries of the Rosary.
- If the recitation of the Rosary is public, the Mysteries of the Rosary must be announced.
- One may gain a partial indulgence for the Rosary's recitation in whole or in part in other circumstances.

A Plenary Indulgence can be gained only once a day (except by those who are in danger of death.) To gain a plenary indulgence one must perform the indulgenced act. Three other conditions must be fulfilled:

1. A sacramental confession
2. Eucharistic Communion
3. Prayers for the Pope's intentions

In addition, one must be free of all attachments to sin, even venial sin. If this complete integrity is not present or if the above conditions are not fulfilled the indulgence is only partial. Both a plenary and partial indulgence may be applied to the dead.

15. CHRIST'S MESSAGE OF MERCY THROUGH ST FAUSTINA

Jesus' words to St. Faustina taken from her Diary:
"I demand from you deeds of mercy which are to arise out of love for Me. You are to show mercy to your neighbors always and everywhere. You must not shrink from this or try to excuse yourself from it **(Faustina, 742)**.

"When a soul approaches Me with trust, I fill it with such an abundance of graces that it cannot contain them within itself, but radiates them to other souls" **(Faustina, 1074)**.

"The greater the sinner, the greater the right he has to My mercy" **(Faustina, 723)**.

"Souls that make an appeal to My mercy delight Me. To such souls I grant even more than they ask. I cannot punish even the greatest sinner if he makes an appeal to My compassion" **(1146)**…"Beg for mercy for the whole world" **(570)**…"No soul that has ever called upon My mercy has ever been disappointed" **(Faustina, 1541)**.

"I have opened My Heart as a living fountain of mercy. Let all souls draw life from it. Let them approach this sea of mercy with trust" **(1520)**…On the cross, the fountain of My mercy was opened wide by the lance for all souls – no one have I excluded! **(1182)**…I am offering people a vessel with which they are to keep coming for graces to the fountain of mercy. That vessel is this image with the signature: "Jesus, I trust in You" **(327)**…"The graces of My mercy are drawn by one vessel only, and that is – trust. The more a soul trusts, the more it will receive" **(Faustina, 1578)**.

"I am Love and Mercy itself **(1074)**…Let no soul fear to draw near to me, even though its sins be as scarlet **(699)**…My mercy is greater than your sins and those of the entire world **(1485)**…I let my Sacred Heart be pierced with a lance, thus opening wide the source of mercy for you. Come, then, with trust to draw graces from this fountain. I never reject a contrite heart **(1485)**…Sooner would heaven and earth turn into nothingness than would My mercy not embrace a trusting soul" **(Faustina, 1777)**.

The above is just a sampling of the many tremendous promises given by our Lord to St. Faustina. These words provide us with a taste for this great devotion of Divine Mercy. The living of this devotion can be summed up in the ABC's of the devotion. That is, we are to: 1. Ask for His mercy; 2. be merciful; 3. trust completely.

The Corporal and Spiritual Works of Mercy

CORPORAL WORKS OF MERCY
1. Feed the hungry. 2. Give drink to the thirsty. 3. Clothe the naked. 4. Shelter the homeless. 5. Comfort the imprisoned. 6. Visit the sick. 7. Bury the dead.

SPIRITUAL WORKS OF MERCY
1. Admonish sinners. 2. Instruct the uninformed. 3. Counsel the doubtful. 4. Comfort the sorrowful. 5. Be patient with those in error. 6. Forgive offenses. 7. Pray for the living and the dead.

Jesus admonishes us through Faustina that in order to receive His infinite Mercy, we must show mercy to others. Jesus explicitly states that he demands deeds of mercy to be done for others out of love for Him. Further, He states that even the greatest faith, without works, is dead.

Essentially, the devotion consists of four significant elements: 1. The Chaplet of Divine Mercy, 2. The three o'clock hour of devotion to the Divine Mercy and the remembrance of His most sorrowful passion, 3. The Novena of Mercy leading up to its conclusion on Divine Mercy Sunday, which falls on the Sunday after Easter, and 4. Veneration of the Sacred Image of Divine Mercy with its inscription, "Jesus, I Trust in You."

The Chaplet of Divine Mercy

St. Faustina experienced a supernatural image or vision of an Angel sent to destroy a certain city due to its tremendous sinfulness. She began imploring God's mercy for the town, but it was to no avail. Suddenly, she found herself immersed in the presence of the Holy Trinity, and she could feel the presence of Jesus within her soul. At the same time, she heard an interior voice reciting the following prayer: **"Eternal Father, I offer You the Body and Blood, Soul and Divinity of your dearly beloved Son, Our Lord Jesus Christ, in atonement for our sins and those of the** whole world; for the sake of His sorrowful Passion, have mercy on us and on the whole world" (Faustina, 476).

As she continued to recite this prayer, the Angel became powerless and weakened, and could not mete out the punishment that the city deserved. The following day, while in the chapel, she again heard an interior voice reciting these words which would constitute the essence of the Chaplet of the Divine Mercy, and she was inspired to recite this chaplet as often as possible for sinners and for the dying. Our Lord made it clear to her that this devotion of "The Chaplet," as Jesus referred to it, was not simply for Faustina to recite, but would become a marvelous devotion that would spread throughout the world through St. Faustina's writings.

What is more, Our Lord revealed tremendous promises associated with the prayer and recitation of the Chaplet of Divine Mercy. Our Lord stated, **"Encourage souls to say the chaplet I have given you (1541)...Whoever will recite it will receive great mercy at the hour of death (687) ... When they say this chaplet in the presence of the dying, I will stand between My Father and the dying person, not as the just Judge but as the Merciful Savior (1541)...Priests will recommend it to sinners as their last hope of salvation. Even if there were a sinner most hardened, if he were to recite this chaplet only once, he would receive grace from My infinite mercy (687)...I desire to grant unimaginable graces to those souls who trust in My mercy (687)...Through the Chaplet you will obtain everything, if what you ask for is compatible with My will"** (1731).

How to Pray the Chaplet

On ordinary Rosary Beads:
1. Pray the "Our Father:" Our Father, Who art in heaven, hallowed be Thy name; Thy kingdom come; Thy will be done on earth as it is in heaven. Give us this day our daily bread; and forgive us our trespasses as we forgive those who trespass against us; and lead us not into temptation, but deliver us from the evil one. Amen.

2. Pray the "Hail Mary:" Hail Mary, full of grace. The Lord is with you. Blessed are you among women, and blessed is the fruit of your womb, Jesus. Holy Mary, Mother of God, pray for us sinners, now and at the hour of our death. Amen.

3. Pray the "Apostles' Creed:" I believe in God, the Father almighty, creator of heaven and earth. I believe in Jesus Christ, His only Son, our Lord. He was conceived by the power of the Holy Spirit, and born of the Virgin Mary. He suffered under Pontius Pilate, was crucified, died, and was buried. He descended to the dead. On the third day He rose again. He ascended into heaven, and is seated at the right hand of the Father. He will come again to judge the living and the dead. I believe in the Holy Spirit, the holy Catholic Church, the communion of saints, the forgiveness of sins, the resurrection of the body, and life everlasting. Amen.

4. On the large bead before each decade: Eternal Father, I offer You the Body, Blood, Soul and Divinity of Your dearly beloved Son, Our Lord Jesus Christ, in atonement for our sins and those of the whole world.

5. On each of the 10 small beads of each decade: For the sake of His sorrowful Passion, have mercy on us and on the whole world.

6. Concluding doxology (after five decades): Holy God, Holy Mighty One, Holy Immortal One, have mercy on us and on the whole world (3x).

The Three O'Clock Hour of Mercy

"At three o'clock implore My mercy especially for sinners; and, if only for a brief moment, immerse yourself in my Passion, particularly in My abandonment at the moment of agony. This is the hour of great mercy for the whole world. I will allow you to enter into my mortal sorrow. In this hour, I will refuse nothing to the soul that makes a request of Me in virtue of My Passion" **(Faustina, 1320).**

FEAST OF DIVINE MERCY
The first Sunday after Easter is the Feast of Mercy. Jesus said, "On that day the very depths of My tender mercy are open. I pour out a whole ocean of graces upon those souls who approach the fount of My mercy. The soul that will go to confession and receive Holy Communion shall obtain complete forgiveness of sins and punishment" **(Faustina, 699).**
Indulgenced by Pope John Paul II, 2002

RECITING THE CHAPLET DURING ADORATION

On the occasion of the Great Jubilee of the year 2000, the Holy Father, Pope John Paul II, by a personally signed parchment, imparted a special Apostolic Blessing "to all the faithful, who during adoration of Our Most Merciful Savior in the Most Blessed Sacrament of the altar will be praying the Divine Mercy Chaplet for the sick and for those throughout the world who will be dying in that hour." The Apostolic Blessing extends indefinitely for all who participate. *Nihil Obstat:* George H. Pearce, S.M., Archbishop of Suva, Fiji. *Imprimatur:* Joseph F. Maguire, Bishop, Springfield, MA, March 16, 1987.

16. SOLEMN ACTS OF TOTAL CONSECRATION TO MARY

Consecration of St Louis de Montfort

O Eternal and Incarnate Wisdom! O sweetest and most adorable Jesus! True God and True Man, only Son of the Eternal Father, and of Mary ever Virgin! I adore Thee profoundly in the bosom and glory of Thy Father during eternity; and I adore Thee also in the virginal bosom of Mary, Thy most worthy Mother, in the time of Thine Incarnation.

I give Thee thanks, that Thou hast annihilated Thyself taking the form of a slave, in order to rescue me from the cruel slavery of the devil. I praise and glorify Thee, that Thou hast been pleased to submit Thyself to Mary, Thy holy Mother, in all things, in order to make me Thy faithful slave through her. But alas! Ungrateful and faithless as I have been, I have not kept the promises which I made so solemnly to Thee in my baptism; I have not fulfilled my obligations; I do not deserve to be called Thy child nor yet Thy slave; and as there is nothing in me which does not merit Thine anger and Thy repulse, I dare no more come by myself before Thy Most Holy and August Majesty.

It is on this account that I have recourse to the Intercession of Thy most holy Mother, whom Thou hast given me for a Mediatrix with Thee. It is by her means that I hope to obtain of Thee contrition, and the pardon of my sins, the acquisition and the preservation of wisdom. I salute Thee, then, O Immaculate Mary living tabernacle of the Divinity, where the Eternal Wisdom willed to be hidden and to be adored by Angels and by men. I hail thee, O Queen of heaven and earth to whose empire everything is subject which is under God. I salute Thee, O sure refuge of sinners, whose mercy fails no one. Hear the desires which I have of the Divine Wisdom; and for that end receive the vows and offerings which my lowness presents to thee.

I, [Name], a faithless sinner, renew and ratify today in thy hands the vows of my Baptism; I renounce for ever Satan, his pomp and works; and I give myself entirely to Jesus Christ, the Incarnate Wisdom, to carry my cross after Him all the days of my life, and to be more faithful to Him than I have ever been before. In the presence of all the heavenly court I choose thee this day for my Mother and Mistress. I deliver and consecrate to thee as Thy slave, my body and soul, my goods, both interior and exterior, and even the value of all my good actions, past present and future; leaving to you the entire and full right of disposing of me, and of all that belongs to me, without exception, according to Thy good pleasure and for the greater glory of God, in time and in eternity.

Receive O gracious Virgin, this little offering of my slavery, in honour of, and in union with, that subjection which the Eternal Wisdom deigned to have thy Maternity, in homage to the power which both of you have over this sinner, and in thanksgiving for the privileges with which the Holy Trinity hath favoured thee. I protest, that I wish, henceforth, as thy true slave, to seek thy honour, and to obey thee in all things.

O admirable Mother, present me to thy Dear Son, as His eternal slave, so that as He hath redeemed me by thee, by thee He may receive me. O Mother of mercy, get me the grace to obtain the true Wisdom of God, and for that end place me in the number of those whom thou lovest, whom thou teachest, whom thou leadest, and whom thou nourishest and protectest, as thy children and thy slaves. O Faithful Virgin, make me in all things so perfect a disciple, imitator and slave of the Incarnate Wisdom, Jesus Christ thy Son, that I may attain, by thy intercession and by thy example, to the fullness of His age on earth, and of His glory in heaven. Amen.

Consecration of St Maximilian Kolbe

Immaculata, Queen of heaven and earth, refuge of sinners and our most loving Mother, God has willed to entrust the entire order of mercy to you. I, N..., a repentant sinner, cast myself at your feet humbly imploring you to take me with all that I am and have, wholly to yourself as your possession and property. Please make of me, of all my powers of soul and body, of my whole life, death and eternity, whatever most pleases you.

If it pleases you, use all that I am and have without reserve, wholly to accomplish what was said of you: "She will crush your head," and, "You alone have destroyed all heresies in the world." Let me be a fit instrument in your immaculate and merciful hands for introducing and increasing your glory to the maximum in all the many strayed and indifferent souls, and thus help extend as far as possible the blessed kingdom of the most Sacred Heart of Jesus. For wherever you enter you obtain the grace of conversion and growth in holiness, since it is through your hands that all graces come to us from the most Sacred Heart of Jesus.

V. Allow me to praise you, O sacred Virgin.
R. Give me strength against your enemies.

Consecration of the Marian Movement of Priests

CONSECRATION TO THE IMMACULATE HEART OF MARY
For the laity
Virgin of Fatima, Mother of Mercy, Queen of Heaven and Earth, Refuge of Sinners, we who belong to the Marian Movement of Priests consecrate ourselves in a very special way to your Immaculate Heart. By this act of consecration we intend to live, with you and through you, all the obligations assumed by our baptismal consecration. We further pledge to bring about in ourselves that interior conversion so urgently demanded by the Gospel, a conversion that will free us of every attachment to ourselves and to easy compromises with the world so that, like you, we may be available only to do always the Will of the Father.

And as we resolve to entrust to you, O Mother most sweet and merciful, our life and vocation as Christians, that you may dispose of it according to your designs of salvation in this hour of decision that weighs upon the world, we pledge to live it according to your desires, especially as it pertains to a renewed spirit of prayer and penance, the fervent participation in the celebration of the Eucharist and in the works of the apostolate, the daily recitation of the holy rosary, and an austere manner of life in keeping with the Gospel, that shall be to all a good example of the observance of the Law of God and the practice of the Christian virtues, especially that of purity.

We further promise you to be united with the Holy Father, with the hierarchy and with our priests, in order thus to set up a barrier to the growing confrontation directed against the Magisterium, that threatens the very foundation of the Church. Under your protection, we want moreover to be apostles of this sorely needed unity of prayer and love for the Pope, on whom we invoke your special protection. And lastly, insofar as is possible, we promise to lead those souls with whom we come in contact to a renewed devotion to you.

Mindful that atheism has caused shipwreck in the faith to a great number of the faithful, that desecration has entered into the holy temple of God, and that evil and sin are spreading more and more throughout the world, we make so bold as to lift our eyes trustingly to you, O Mother of Jesus and our merciful and powerful Mother, and we invoke again today and await from you the salvation of all your children, O clement, O loving, O sweet Virgin Mary (with ecclesiastical approval).

17. CONCLUSION

In conclusion, here is part of the final message given by Our Lady to Fr. Gobbi:

All Has Been Revealed to You
Milan, Italy; December 31, 1997

"All has been revealed to you: my plan has been prophetically announced to you at Fatima, and during these years, I have been carrying it out through my Marian Movement of Priests. This has been revealed to you in its gradual preparation. This century of yours, which is about to end, has been placed under the sign of a strong power conceded to my Adversary. Thus, humanity has been led astray by the error of theoretical and practical atheism; in the place of God, idols have been built which everyone adores: pleasure, money, amusements, power, pride, and impurity."

"Truly Satan, with the cup of lust, has succeeded in seducing all the nations of the earth. He has replaced love with hatred; communion with division; justice with many injustices; peace with continuous war. In fact this entire century has been spent under the sign of cruel and bloody wars, which have claimed millions of innocent victims. So then, the Most Holy Trinity has decreed that your century be placed under the sign of my powerful, maternal and extraordinary presence. Thus, at Fatima, I pointed out the way along which humanity must journey for its return to the Lord: that of conversion, prayer and penance. And as a safe refuge, I offered you my Immaculate Heart."

"All has been revealed to you: my plan has been pointed out to you even in its painful realization. Humanity has fallen under the domination of Satan and of his great power, exercised with the satanic and Masonic forces; my Church has become obscured by his smoke which has penetrated into it. Errors are being taught and propagated, causing many to lose true faith in Christ and in His Gospel; the holy Law of God is openly violated; sin is committed and often even justified, and thus the light of grace and of the divine presence is lost; unity is deeply split apart by a strong contestation directed against the Magisterium, and especially against the Pope; and the wound caused by painful lacerations becomes ever wider...."

"All has been revealed to you: my plan has been foretold to you especially in its wonderful and victorious fulfillment. I have announced to you the triumph of my Immaculate Heart in the world. In the end, my Immaculate Heart will triumph. This will come about in the greatest triumph of Jesus, who will bring into the world his glorious reign of love, of justice and of peace, and will make all things new....With the love of a Mother who, during these years, has been listened to, followed and glorified by you, I bless you all in the name of the Father, and of the Son, and of the Holy Spirit" (Gobbi, Message 604).

APPENDIX A

The Morning Offering

The Morning Offering is, essentially, an offering of all the day's prayers, works, joys and especially sufferings to the Heavenly Father in union with Jesus' perfect offering of Himself, renewed each day throughout the world in the celebration of the Holy Sacrifice of the Mass. In the Mass, the Holy Spirit, in a wholly mystical and supernatural fashion, truly makes present the sacrifice of Christ on Calvary. Most Christians do not consider the reality that when they are participating in the Mass, they are quite literally kneeling at the foot of the Cross, and uniting the sacrifices and sufferings of their lives to Christ's perfect oblation to the Father on behalf of souls.

Few realize that through our baptismal consecration, we are made sharers in the Priestly, Prophetic, and Kingly functions of Christ. Christ is the one and only High Priest who offered the perfect sacrifice of Himself on the altar of the cross, where He was both Priest and Victim. Through our Baptism, we are enabled to offer spiritual sacrifices to the Father through, with and in Christ, specifically in the renewal of Christ's perfect redemptive act made truly present in the Liturgy of the Eucharist at the moment of Consecration. As baptized Christians, we are called to unite our sacrifices and sufferings to Christ's offering, renewed each day in the mass, and thereby participate in the distribution of grace and mercy to the human family. Thus, we are co-redeemers with Christ, as St. Paul states, "In my sufferings, I make up for what is lacking in the sufferings of Christ." St. Paul doesn't mean to imply that there is anything whatever lacking in the perfect, redemptive act of Christ. Rather, he is underscoring the reality that through our participation in the common, royal priesthood of Christ that was conferred upon us in baptism, we have the right, privilege and obligation of "offering up" our sufferings in union with Christ.

The Virgin Mary is the perfect example of one who, in a wholly singular way participates intimately in the passion of Christ, her Son, and is therefore referred to as the Co-Redemptrix. The co- in no way implies equality with Christ; rather, Mary's participation in the salvific action of Christ in completely subordinate to and dependant on the work of redemption wrought by Christ. Yet, she, more than any other living creature, cooperated in a profound and mystical fashion in the passion, and participated in meriting grace - life - for the human family. Therefore she is our Spiritual Mother in the order of Grace, and it is only fitting that she who participated in the meriting of Grace would also participate in the distribution of that Grace. Thus, in addition to being the Co-Redemptrix, she is also the Mediatrix of all graces. This is to say that every grace that comes to us from God comes through the willed intercession of Mary.

It is precisely for this reason that the most sublime of all devotions is that of total consecration to Mary. She is most able to exercise her role as Mediatrix with respect to those souls who've entrusted themselves completely to her via a heartfelt consecration to her. For, how can a mother nourish a child who puts up resistance to her? We must be docile in her arms, imitating Christ who became a little child and entrusted Himself completely to the care of Mary. Essential aspects of living our consecration to Mary include the daily recitation of her prayer, the Holy Rosary, daily renewal of our act of consecration, and the patient acceptance of the cross that God has willed for us to carry for the sake of our own sanctification and in atonement for the sins of the world. Thus, we can now see how the morning/daily offering and daily participation in the Holy Sacrifice of the Mass are essential components to living our total consecration to Mary. What follows is a daily offering that can be prayed at the beginning of each day as an exercise of our royal priesthood:

MORNING OFFERING PRAYER

Eternal Father, in union with the Immaculate Heart of Mary to whom I am totally consecrated, I offer all the prayers, works, joys and especially sufferings of this day and of my whole life, past, present and future, in union with Christ's perfect offering of Himself renewed this day, throughout the world, in the Holy Sacrifice of the Mass, for all the intentions of the Sacred Hearts of Jesus and Mary, for the Holy Father and his intentions; for all Bishops and Priests; for good Priestly vocations; in atonement for the sins of my whole life; for the intentions of my relatives, friends and all persons who have asked for my prayers; for the conversion of sinners; for the liberty and exaltation of the Church; and finally for the grace of a happy, holy death in the arms of Jesus and Mary. Amen.

APPENDIX B

The Life Offering

(Source: Booklet by the same title, published by Two Hearts Books and Publishers):

Mary, our Heavenly Mother, implores those who receive Holy Communion daily, or at least weekly, to offer their lives for the greater glory of God and the salvation of souls, that the souls of sinners may not be damned but receive, at least at their last hour, the graces of eternal life.

The Five Promises of Mary to Those Who Offer Their Lives to Her:
1. Their names will be written in the Hearts of Jesus and Mary, inflamed by love.
2. Their life offering, together with the infinite merits of Jesus, can save many souls from damnation. All souls who live until the end of the world will benefit from their life offering.
3. None of their family members will go to hell, even if it seems otherwise, because they will receive, in the depths of their souls, the grace of sincere contrition before the soul departs from their bodies.
4. On the day they offer their lives, their loved ones suffering in purgatory will be released.
5. I will be with them at the hour of their death. They will not know purgatory. I will carry their souls straight to the presence of the Glorious Trinity, where they will live with me in a special place created by God and will rejoice forever.

The Life Offering Prayer
My dear Jesus, before the Holy Trinity, Our Heavenly Mother, and the whole Heavenly Court, united with your most precious Blood and your sacrifice on Calvary, I hereby offer my whole life to the intention of your Sacred Heart and to the Immaculate Heart of Mary. Together with my life, I place at your disposal all Holy Masses, all my Holy Communions, all my good deeds, all my sacrifices, and the sufferings of my entire life for the adoration and supplication of the Holy Trinity, for unity in our Holy Mother Church, for the Holy Father and priests, for good priestly vocations, and for all souls until the end of the world. O my Jesus, please accept my life sacrifice and my offerings and give me your grace that I may persevere obediently until my death. Amen.

This life offering must be made with a humble heart, firm resolution, and clear intent. All prayer, good deeds, suffering, and work done with a pure intention have great merit, if it is offered together with the merits, the sufferings, and the Blood of Jesus Christ. It is recommended that you make this life offering as soon as you feel ready, and to renew it from time to time.

Excerpts from the messages received by the privileged soul:

Our Heavenly Mother: "My children who offer your lives, make the act of contrition every day! Make it not only for yourselves but for all men. This will continually weaken the power of evil to tempt and will help all souls to free themselves from the slavery to sin."

Prayer of Contrition

O my Jesus, I love you over and above everything! For the love of you I am sorry for all my sins. O merciful love, I ask pardon for the sins of the whole world. United with the Immaculate Heart of our Heavenly Mother, I ask pardon for all my sins and for all the sins of my brothers and sisters that have been and will committed until the end of the world. My dear Jesus, united with your Holy Wounds, I offer my life to the Eternal Father according to the intention of the Sorrowful Mother. Virgin Mary, Queen of heaven and earth, Mediatrix of all grace and mercy, our only refuge and hope, pray for us!

Our Lady (to those who offer their lives): "If the Eternal Father chooses to give a soul the grace of being among the elect, He will order that soul to become similar to His only-begotten Son while on earth; but in what way should this soul be like His Son? In love and acceptance of sufferings. If you follow your Jesus in these two ways, then the Eternal Father will recognize His Holy Son in you."

"Souls chosen by the Eternal Father to offer their lives must strive to save as many other souls as possible. This can be done through fervent prayer, through the practice of love, through meekness, humility and self-denial, but above all through the patient acceptance of sufferings. I believe that my Motherly Heart will find among my children souls who love God with the love of the martyrs."

"My children, even during the greatest trials, hold my motherly hand with unbounded trust. Come together with me to the Sacred Heart of Jesus: He is your strength on your earthly pilgrimage. Thus, strengthened by Him daily, you will march toward your eternal dwelling place of happiness where you will recognize each other in glorious ecstasy, you who sacrificed your lives for the glory of God and the salvation of souls. Then my Holy Son will embrace you to His flaming Heart, and He will immerse you in the ecstasy of the united love of the Trinity. In this state of eternal bliss, you will rejoice forever, together with those souls who were able to gain eternal life because of your selfless life sacrifice."

"Hope and love, because God is with you. My children, each offered life is pleasing to God. Therefore, do not limit your sacrifice. This should be your life slogan: Give more and love better!"

"Once you surrender yourself to great sufferings of either body or soul, the experience can be a fountain of immeasurable grace. You can pay for the sins of your life, or for the things you have failed to do. Or if this has already been paid, then the merit of your patient sufferings can be applied to conversion of hardened sinners. By that you can glorify God. The souls you save by your obedient acceptance of sufferings may even become saints. When the weight of suffering lies heavily on you, whether illness or suffering in the soul, always remember that you are just a pilgrim on this earth. Beyond the grave there is a wonderful world that was prepared by God for His faithful children, where your happiness will be greater than that which your patient and obedient sufferings could possibly merit. As it is written: your soul will forever be immersed in such happiness that eye has not seen, ear has not heard, neither has it entered into the heart of man, what things God has prepared for those that love Him (1 Cor. 2:9)."

"No matter how heavy your suffering on earth, it will last but a short time. Rejoice while you suffer, because you are proceeding toward a sure goal, and at the end of this road, your Heavenly Mother is waiting for you to embrace you with the eternal love of the Trinity…My children! I am calling you to apostolic privilege. You are chosen to suffer martyrdom of the heart for the sins of others. And by this voluntary life sacrifice – coming from your good heart – God will be able to pour out the flood of His mercy. Think about that!"

"My beloved children! If you carry patiently the little thorn from the cross of my Son that He has given to you, you can save countless souls from eternal damnation. Thus, holding the hand of your Heavenly Mother, you too will partake in the work of redemption. My Children! Do not ask for sufferings, but always accept with humility and selflessness those that the Lord hands to you. . . My children! Give everything to me and I will give everything to my Holy Son, united with my interceding prayers. I am the Woman who sets slaves free."

"My beloved Children: My Holy Son finished the work of redemption. His own sacrifice was enough, but He left a little part to you. He calls and elects certain souls to share His sacrifice in an intimate union with Him. He suffered for the glory of God and for the salvation of souls. It is a joy for my Son to see Himself in them."

The seer (April 20, 1978): When I was in Church once, I rejoiced to see many present offering their lives faithfully to God's will. My spiritual director led the offering prayer. I wondered whether these people would fulfill their life offering. Is it enough to give oneself once? Will these people live accordingly or even think about it later? Then I heard Jesus addressing me: "My child, if someone performs the life offering only once – do you understand, only once, once in an elevated moment of grace, when in his soul the flame of heroic offering will be lit – this soul has determined his whole life even if he never thinks about it again. He will be the property of the most Holy Hearts. Time does not exist before my Father. He sees the life of a person in its wholeness. Even if someone has made some other offering before, this life offering will include everything, and it is above all. This will be the crown, the most beautiful adornment, for that soul. This will determine the place and rank of nobility of this soul in the eternal kingdom!"

Jesus (Sept. 24, 1971), Feast of Our Lady of Ransom: "My little apostles! My Mother is the most beautiful Temple of God. She is the most beautiful among all My living Temples. On her altar is the throne of the Trinity. This altar is adorned with the most beautiful red roses grown under My cross, together with the lilies of immaculate purity. The sanctuary lamp of this altar is fueled with the oil of humility, and it is surrounded with the candles of never-ending selfless love, and the lights of these candles illuminate this altar for every soul. In this temple the tired will find rest, those who cry will find consolation, sinners will find conversion, and the ambitious will find maternal love. Visit often this most beautiful temple of God. Through this temple, you will find the grace that will enable you to reach the eternal kingdom. My children! Even one soul who puts himself on the sacrificial altar, prompted by the love of Me and the love of his brothers, will magnify a hundredfold the Glory of God and the gladness of My Mother. Stand up, My children, with great fervor!"

"My children! The fate of My Church is always in My Heart, since I promised that the gates of hell will not prevail against her. I still have many good and true priests, but many have discarded the cloth of election. In place of the unfaithful, disloyal priests, I created My fishers of souls! These are the priests of the Hearts of Jesus and Mary, who are called by the Lord of the harvest to work quietly for souls and for the glory of God. Even if there is a shortage of priests – and so it seems – a multitude of souls will escape damnation, because instead of disloyal priests there stands the life offering love!" *Nihil Obstat:* P. Alberto Valenzuel, S.J. *Imprimatur:* Pbro. Agustin Gutierez de la Torre, Vicar General of the Archdiocese of Guadalajara, 12 June, 1988.

APPENDIX C

Promises of the Immaculate Heart of Mary

Five First Saturdays Devotion of Reparation to the Immaculate Heart of Mary and the Tremendous Promise of Salvation

Our Lady spoke this tremendous promise to Sr. Lucy, one of the three visionaries of Fatima, stating that she would secure all the graces necessary for salvation for anyone who performed the following devotion with the intention of making reparation to her Immaculate Heart:

"See, my daughter, my Heart encircled by thorns with which ungrateful men pierce it at every moment by their blasphemies and ingratitude. Do you, at least, strive to console me. Tell them that I promise to assist at the hour of death with the graces necessary for salvation all those who, in order to make reparation to me, on the First Saturday of five successive months, go to confession, receive Holy Communion, say five decades of the Rosary, and keep me company for a quarter of an hour, meditating on the fifteen mysteries of the Rosary."

APPENDIX D

Original Prayer to St Michael the Archangel

WRITTEN BY POPE LEO XIII

"O Glorious Prince of the heavenly host, St. Michael the Archangel, defend us in the battle and in the terrible warfare that we are waging against the principalities and powers, against the rulers of this world of darkness, against the evil spirits. Come to the aid of man, whom Almighty God created immortal, made in His own image and likeness, and redeemed at a great price from the tyranny of Satan."

"Fight this day the battle of the Lord, together with the holy angels, as already thou hast fought the leader of the proud angels, Lucifer, and his apostate host, who were powerless to resist thee, nor was there place for them any longer in Heaven. That cruel, ancient serpent, who is called the devil or Satan who seduces the whole world, was cast into the abyss with his angels. Behold, this primeval enemy and slayer of men has taken courage. Transformed into an angel of light, he wanders about with all the multitude of wicked spirits, invading the earth in order to blot out the name of God and of His Christ, to seize upon, slay and cast into eternal perdition souls destined for the crown of eternal glory. This wicked dragon pours out, as a most impure flood, the venom of his malice on men of depraved mind and corrupt heart, the spirit of lying, of impiety, of blasphemy, and the pestilent breath of impurity, and of every vice and iniquity."

"These most crafty enemies have filled and inebriated with gall and bitterness the Church, the spouse of the immaculate Lamb, and have laid impious hands on her most sacred possessions. In the Holy Place itself, where the See of Holy Peter and the Chair of Truth has been set up as the light of the world, they have raised the throne of their abominable impiety, with the iniquitous design that when the Pastor has been struck, the sheep may be."

"Arise then, O invincible Prince, bring help against the attacks of the lost spirits to the people of God, and give them the victory. They venerate thee as their protector and patron; in thee holy Church glories as her defense against the malicious power of hell; to thee has God entrusted the souls of men to be established in heavenly beatitude. Oh, pray to the God of peace that He may put Satan under our feet, so far conquered that he may no longer be able to hold men in captivity and harm the Church. Offer our prayers in the sight of the Most High, so that they may quickly find mercy in the sight of the Lord; and vanquishing the dragon, the ancient serpent, who is the devil and Satan, do thou again make him captive in the abyss, that he may no longer seduce the nations. Amen."

V. Behold the Cross of the Lord; be scattered ye hostile powers.
R. The Lion of the tribe of Judah, the root of David, has conquered.
V. Let Thy mercies be upon us, O Lord.
R. As we have hoped in Thee.
V. O Lord, hear my prayer.
R. And let my cry come unto Thee.

"Let us pray: O God, the Father of our Lord Jesus Christ, we call upon Thy holy Name, and as supplicants, we implore Thy clemency, that by the intercession of Mary, ever Virgin Immaculate and our Mother, and of the glorious St. Michael the Archangel, Thou wouldst deign to help us against Satan and all the other unclean spirits who wander about the world for the injury of the human race and the ruin of souls. Amen."

(Source: Roman Raccolta, July 23, 1898, supplement approved July 31, 1902, London: Burnes, Oates & Washbourne Ltd., 1935, 12th edition).

APPENDIX E

Blessing of Salt and Water

PRIEST VESTS IN SURPLICE AND PURPLE STOLE
P: Our help is in the name of the Lord.
R: Who made heaven and earth.

Exorcism of Salt (necessary for the Exorcism of Water):
P: O salt, creature of God, I exorcise you by the living (+) God, by the true (+) God, by the holy (+) God, by the God who ordered you to be poured into the water by Elisha the prophet, so that its life-giving powers might be restored. I exorcise you so that you may become a means of salvation for believers, that you may bring health of soul and body to all who make use of you, and that you may put to flight and drive away from the places where you are sprinkled; every apparition, villainy, turn of devilish deceit, and every unclean spirit; adjured by him who will come to judge the living and the dead and the world by fire.
R: Amen.
P: Let us pray. Almighty and everlasting God, we humbly implore you, in your immeasurable kindness and love, to bless (+) this salt which you created and gave to the use of mankind, so that it may become a source of health for the minds and bodies of all who make use of it. May it rid whatever it touches or sprinkles of all uncleanness, and protect it from every assault of evil spirits. Through Christ our Lord.
R: Amen.

Exorcism of Water:
P: O water, creature of God, I exorcise you in the name of God the Father (+) Almighty, and in the name of Jesus (+) Christ His Son, our Lord, and in the power of the Holy (+) Spirit. I exorcise you so that you may put to flight all the power of the enemy, and be able to root out and supplant that enemy with his apostate angels, through the power of our Lord Jesus Christ, who will come to judge the living and the dead and the world by fire.
R: Amen.
P: Let us pray. O God, for the salvation of mankind, you built your greatest mysteries on this substance, water. In your kindness, hear our prayers and pour down the power of your blessing (+) into this element, made ready for many kinds of purifications. May this, your creature, become an agent of divine grace in the service of your mysteries, to drive

away evil spirits and dispel sickness, so that everything in the homes and other buildings of the faithful that is sprinkled with this water, may be rid of all uncleanness and freed from every harm. Let no breath of infection and no disease-bearing air remain in these places. May the wiles of the lurking enemy prove of no avail. Let whatever might menace the safety and peace of those who live here be put to flight by the sprinkling of this water, so that the health obtained by calling upon your holy name, may be made secure against all attack. Through Christ our Lord.

R: Amen.

(Priest pours exorcised salt into the water, in the form of a cross).

P: May a mixture of salt and water now be made, in the name of the Father, and of the (+) Son, and of the Holy Spirit.

R: Amen.

P: The Lord be with you.

R: And with your spirit.

P: Let us pray. O God, Creator unconquerable, invincible King, Victor ever-glorious, you hold in check the forces bent on dominating us. You overcome the cruelty of the raging enemy, and in your power you beat down the wicked foe. Humbly and fearfully do we pray to you, O Lord, and we ask you to look with favor on this salt and water which you created. Shine on it with the light of your kindness. Sanctify it by the dew of your love, so that, through the invocation of your holy name, wherever this water and salt is sprinkled, it may turn aside every attack of the unclean spirit, and dispel the terrors of the poisonous serpent. And wherever we may be, make the Holy Spirit present to us, who now implore your mercy. Through Christ our Lord.

R: Amen.

(Source: http://www.catholictools.com/exorcism-blessing-for-water-and-salt/)

APPENDIX F

Petition for Papal Declaration of Mary as Co-Redemptrix, Mediatrix and Advocate

I encourage you to prayerfully consider copying and mailing the following petition to His Holiness, Pope Benedict XVI, for the solemn papal definition of the Virgin Mary as the Spiritual Mother of All Peoples, Co-redemptrix, Mediatrix of all graces and Advocate. You may also compose a petition in your own words, and mail it to the address listed below. You may include your name and address at the end of the petition.

To His Holiness, Pope Benedict XVI
Apostolic Palace
00120 Vatican City State
Europe

Your Holiness:
In a spirit of filial love and obedience, we, as members of the People of God, wish to humbly bring before you our petition and prayer for the solemn papal definition of the revealed role of Mary most holy as the Spiritual Mother of all peoples under its three principal aspects as Co-redemptrix, Mediatrix of all graces, and Advocate.

We firmly believe, Holy Father, that the solemn papal declaration of the Blessed Virgin Mary as the Spiritual Mother of all humanity in her roles which God has given her as Co-redemptrix, Mediatrix of all graces, and Advocate will bring great graces to the Church and the world by an explicit solemn recognition of her maternal role on the part of the Church, and thus allowing her to exercise fully the motherly gift which Jesus Christ gave to humanity from the cross: "Woman, behold, your son!... Behold, your mother!" (Jn. 19:26-27). We believe that this dogmatic proclamation will also further the authentic ecumenical mission of the Church by proclaiming the revealed truth about Mary, who collaborated in an altogether unique way in the work of our redemption in a manner that was completely subordinate to and dependent upon Jesus Christ, the one divine Redeemer of the human race.

In view of the many serious crises presently facing the entire human family, including war, terrorism, moral decline, and natural disaster, we humbly request that you solemnly declare the dogma of Mary as the

Spiritual Mother all peoples, specifying that she is the Co-redemptrix, Mediatrix of all graces, and Advocate, and thus to provide for the full actuality of her motherly roles of intercession for humanity, which we believe will effect a profound historic and continuing grace for the Church and for the world.

(Source: http://fifthmariandogma.com/)

WORKS CITED

1. "A Detailed Catholic Examination of Conscience." Beginning Catholic.com 2006. 9 May, 2011 <http://www.beginningcatholic.com/catholic-examination-of-conscience.html>

2. Bergeron, Henri-Paul. Brother Andre, The Wonder Man of Mount Royal. St. Joseph' Oratory. 1988.

3. Clurnet, Leon. "La Salette." The Catholic Encyclopedia. Vol. 9, New York: Robert Appleton Company, 1910. 9 May, 2011 <http://www.newadvent.org/cathen/09008b.htm>

4. De Domenico, Dominic. True Devotion to Saint Joseph and the Church. New Hope: St. Gabriel Press.

5. De Montfort, Louis. True Devotion to Mary. Rockford: Tan. 1985.

6. Denis, Gabriel. The Reign of Jesus Through Mary. Bay Shore: Montfort Pub. 1995.

7. "Exorcism Blessing for Water and Salt." CatholicTools.com. 9 May, 2011 <http://www.catholictools.com/exorcism-blessing-for-water-and-salt/>

8. Gobbi, Don Stefano. The Triumph, The Second Coming and the Eucharistic Reign. St. Francis, ME: Marian Movement of Priests. 2000.

9. Gobbi, Don Stefano. To the Priests, Our Lady's Beloved Sons. Marian Movement of Priests: St. Francis, ME. 2009

10. John Paul, Pope. "An active silence of service to the Holy Family." L'Osservatore Romano 27 March 1996.

11. John Paul, Pope. "Catechism of the Catholic Church." The Holy See. Liberia Editrice Vaticana. 2003. The Roman Catholic Church. 9 May, 2011 <http://www.vatican.va/archive/ENG0015/_INDEX.HTM#fonte

12. Joseph, Aaron. In the Spirit of St. Joseph. Enfield: St. Joseph's Place Pub. 1997.

13. Kolbe, Maximilian. Aim Higher. Libertyville, IL: Marytown Press, 2007.

14. Kowalska, M. Faustina. Divine Mercy in my Soul. Stockbridge, MA: Marian Press. 1987.

15. Leo XIII, Pope. Roman Raccolta. London. Burnes, Oates & Washbourne, 1935.

16. Life Offering: To the Sacred Heart through the Immaculate Heart. Mountain View, CA. Two Hearts Books and Publishers. 1993.

17. Lumen Gentium, Dogmatic Constitution on the Church. Boston: Pauline Books. 1964.

18. Manteau-Bonamy, H.M. Immaculate Conception and the Holy Spirit. Libertyville: Prow. 1977.

19. Melanson, Paul Anthony. "One Step Closer to a Fifth Marian Dogma?" Blogspot. 30 May, 2009. 9 May, 2011 <http://lasalettejourney.blogspot.com/2009/05/one-step-closer-to-fifth-marian-dogma.html>

20. Miravalle, Mark, S.T.D. Introduction to Mary. Santa Barbara: Queenship Pub. 1993.

21. Miravalle, Mark, S.T.D. "Petition for Papal Proclamation of Mary, Coredemptrix, Mediatrix and Advocate." Fifth Marian Dogma.com. Vox Populi. 9 May, 2011 <http://www.fifthmariandogma.com>

22. Miravalle, Mark, S.T.D. "Why Now is the Time for a Dogma of Mary Coredemptrix." FifthMarianDogma.com. Mark I. Miravalle. 31 Oct., 2002. Zenit. 9 May, 2011 <http://www.fifthmariandogma.com/index.php?option=com_content&view=articleco-redemptrix&catid=105:articles&Itemid=582>

23. Peerdman, Ida. "The Lady of All Nations – Apparitions to Ida Peerdman in Amsterdam." Circle of Prayer. Mary Mullins. 2002. Moytura. 9 May, 2011 <http://www.circleofprayer.com/theladyofallnations.html>

24. Redemptoris Custos. St. Paul Books. 1989.

25. Redemptoris Mater. Boston: St. Paul Books. 1987.

26. Ritchie, John. "Quotes about the Rosary by Our Lady, Popes, and Saints." Catholic Campus Watch. 2011. 9 May, 2011. <http://www.catholiccampuswatch.blogspot.com/2010/11/quotes-of-our-lady-popes-and-saints-html>

27. Smolenski, Stanley, Rev. "St. Joseph's Place in the Third Millennium" Enfield: St. Martha Church. 1997.

28. "The Apocalypse of St. John (Revelation)." Douay-Rheims Catholic Bible Online. Tan Books. 1971. 9, May, 2011 <http://www.drbo.org/chapter/73012.htm>

29. The Roman Catholic Church. "The Third Secret of Fatima." The Holy See. The Vatican. 9 May, 2011 <http://www.vatican.va/roman_curia/congregations/cfaith/documents/rc_con_cfaith_doc_20000626_message_fatima_en.html>

30. "The Scriptural Rosary." Rosary Army. 2011. 9 May, 2011 <http://www.rosaryarmy.com/?page_id=585>

31. "The Secret in Three Parts: The Second Part." The Fatima Network. 1996-2010. 9 May, 2011 <http://www.fatima.org/essentials/message/tspart2.asp>

32. "The Vision of Pope Leo XIII." St. Joseph's Catholic Church. 9 May, 2011 <http://www.stjosephschurch.net/leoxiii.htm>

33. Thompson, Edward. The Life and Glories of St. Joseph. Rockville: Tan. 1980.

34. Trigilio, John & Kenneth Brighenti. "The Seven Deadly Sins of the Catholic Church." Dummies.com. Wiley Pub. 2011. 9 May, 2011 http://www.dummies.com/how-to/content/the-seven-deadly-sins-of-the-catholic-church.html

35. Yasuda, Teiji. "Sr. Agnes Sasagawa." EWTN. 9 May, 2011 <http://www.ewtn.com/library/mary/akita/htm>

ABOUT THE AUTHOR

Jayson M. Brunelle, M.Ed., CAGS, earned his Bachelor of Arts degree in Philosophy and Theology from Franciscan University of Steubenville, having graduated Magna Cum Laude. Mr. Brunelle continued his studies in Counseling Psychology and in Clinical Mental Health Counseling at Springfield College, earning there a Master of Education and a Certificate of Advanced Graduate Studies respectively.

Mr. Brunelle's writings have been featured in numerous professional publications, including *Homiletic and Pastoral Review*, *Petrus National Pastoral Monthly* and *Lay Witness*. He was invited to present two articles, one of which he was primary author, at the *8th International Congress on Constructivism and Psychotherapy* held in Monopoli-Bari, Italy in 2003. Mr. Brunelle has worked as a clinical mental health counselor, an adjunct professor, a chaplain and a writer. He is based in Western Massachusetts. He is also webmaster of the blog, www.marianapostolate.com and founder of Marian Apostolate. His professional website is www.jaysonbrunelle.com and he can be contacted via email at jaysonmbrunelle@gmail.com.